The Persistent Problems of Psychology

The
Persistent Problems
of
Psychology

by

Robert B. MacLeod

DUQUESNE UNIVERSITY PRESS, PITTSBURGH

1975

Distributed by Humanities Press, Atlantic Highlands

First printing

Printed in the United States of America

Library of Congress Cataloging in Publication Data

MacLeod, Robert Brodie, 1907—1972.
  The persistent problems of psychology.

  "An unfinished book . . . a table of contents of
the intended volume is included."
  Includes index.
  1. Psychology—History. I. Title.
[DNLM: 1. Psychology—History. BF81 M165p]
BF81.M28 1975   150'.9   75-15635
ISBN 0-391-00393-3

Duquesne University Press
University Hall
Pittsburgh, Pennsylvania 15219

Contents

v

PART II.

The Renaissance and Its Implications

PART III.

Psychology Becomes a Science

Preface

ROBERT BRODIE MACLEOD spent a large part of his professional life making it possible for other people to do their work. His chairmanship of three distinguished psychology departments—at Swarthmore College, McGill University, and Cornell University—over a period of some twenty years cut deeply into his time for scholarly work, while enabling his colleagues to get on with their research. He was a dedicated teacher, and the work with students again took precedence over his own research. To arouse interest in psychology and its history, to explore issues, to hone minds, to offer a model of serious, responsible, and passionate scholarship constituted MacLeod's conception of teaching, a conception as demanding in time and energy as it was productive of young psychologists. His many and varied professional activities—in the American Psychological Association, in helping to shape psychological education in Canada, in his service on numerous editorial boards, and so on—all contributed to raising the standards of psychological teaching and publication, but all took their toll on his working time.

The result is that this book is unfinished. MacLeod had been working on it intermittently for many years, and he used chapters of it in his courses in the history of psychology. He did not live to complete it. But an unfinished book by Robert MacLeod is better than no book at all; and, even incomplete, this one will fill a gap in the literature available for the teaching of the history of psychology. The volume is a history of man's thinking about himself from the earliest times up to the development of scientific psychology. Fortunately, the author began at the beginning. Most students come to the history of psychology without the background in intellectual history that would make it comprehensible to them. The first few chapters of this book supply that background in a way that few other sources could do, since few scholars possess the philosophical erudition of Professor MacLeod combined with his broad knowledge of contemporary psychology. Each period, ancient, Renaissance, nineteenth century, is shown against the social and scientific background of its times. The prehistory of psychology is presented always with a view to the contemporary scene, so that the reader will see its relevance to today's psychological problems. This is the book of a contemplative, erudite, and lively thinker, written so clearly that it will engage the interests of the beginning student, and so faithfully that it will refresh, or perhaps add a new perspective to, the knowledge of his elders.

The inclusion of both the nineteenth century background and a short history of associationism provides essential context for an understanding of contemporary psychology. There is a brief fragment on hedonism which, although incomplete, will fill a gap for present-day psychology, which tends to ignore these issues or take them for granted. Part of a chapter on early laboratory psychology raises questions which should not be overlooked by the modern reader.

From here on the instructor is on his own. But a table of contents of the intended volume is included, so that he may, if he wishes, build his course in the history of psychology on the structure provided by Professor MacLeod. Instructors of courses in systems of psychology will find that this volume provides an indispensable background against which to view the modern period.

One of the exceptional merits of this book is that Professor MacLeod knew so much more than the rest of us. This, his last contribution to psychology, is a worthy postscript to a career of dedicated scholarship and teaching.

Mary Henle
New School for Social Research

Michael Wertheimer
University of Colorado

January 31, 1975

Introduction

THE PERSISTENT PROBLEMS OF PSYCHOLOGY introduces the field and simply and clearly sets before the reader the inescapable problems of philosophy and psychology, the traditional views of man, and the basic assumptions contained in the major approaches to psychology. It is the first discussion which gives to historical psychology *conceptual* continuity and cohesiveness. Primarily a history of the major pervasive ideas and issues which have concerned man since the dawn of reasoned thought and discourse, its continuity is assured by the very challenge of the persistent puzzles rather than by "chronology" or by "great thinkers". Ideas move forward, metamorphose, and generate new ideas—personalities are left behind.

Professor MacLeod is a thinker who has the foresight and bravery to remind us of the viable wisdom of the past. In one of his last papers he writes: "The history of ideas is the history of *ideas*, not a history of people. . . . Ideas must move on."[1] Ideas prevail over events, outliving the past and the people who remember it. He believes that the study of these ideas nourishes conceptual clarification, intellectual and moral emancipation, and melioration of ascending man.

An overview of Professor MacLeod's ideas provides a pertinent perspective for *The Persistent Problems of Psychology*. Initially, some suggestion of his intellectual heritage, followed by some motifs of the content and method of his thinking, writing, and teaching may

1. R. B. MacLeod, "Newtonian and Darwinian conceptions of man; and some alternatives." *Journal of the History of Behavioral Sciences 6:* (1970) 208.

enhance our appreciation of the book.[2] Specific commentary on *The Persistent Problems* follows: six themes are differentiated in order to illustrate his thinking in preparing and writing the book. Finally, some speculation about the direction he might have taken is presented.

PERSPECTIVE: WHAT PSYCHOLOGY HAS BEEN AND WHAT IT CAN BECOME

MacLeod does more than remind us of the wisdom of the past. He personally models several philosopher-scientists whose common approach is tenacious questioning of established dogma. As a philosopher and teacher MacLeod's demeanor is closest to Socrates'. One remembers, understands, and grows best by means of self-discovered truth. As a scientist he emulates Galileo. The facts of careful and repeated observation, uninfluenced by presuppositions as to what one must find, speak more clearly than any intimidating and time-honored partyline. As a methodologist he follows Descartes. No set of spoken or unspoken assumptions, beliefs, or values is safe from or impervious to probing, inspecting, and reinspecting; yet the self of conscious experience (*cogito*) seemingly remains an inevitable basis of knowing. As an experimenter he is closest to David Katz.[3] His relation to Gestalt psychology is unmistakable. No problem of human experience or behavior is intractable or ingenuity-proof, and few can fail to profit from unbiased curiosity, guided by disciplined naivete—by an initial fresh look at the subtle and penetrating psycho-

---

2. Other aspects of his life, career, and contributions are already part of the written offering by his friends and students:

Giorgi, A., "In Memoriam: Robert B. MacLeod (1907–1972)." *Journal of Phenomenological Psychology 3:* (1972) iii-iv.

Kelly, B., "A personal remembrance." In: *The MacLeod Symposium*, D. Krech (Ed.). (Ithaca, New York: Cornell University, Department of Psychology, 1973), pp. 127–128.

Bronfenbrenner, U., Ryan, T., and Gibson, J., "Robert Brodie MacLeod." In: *Memorial Statements: Cornell University, 1971–1972.* (Ithaca, New York: Cornell University Press, 1973), pp. 18–20.

Wertheimer, M., "Robert Brodie MacLeod (1907–1972)." *Journal of the History of the Behavioral Sciences 9:* (1973) 287–299.

3. Katz was one of MacLeod's mentors; c.f., "David Katz, 1884–1953." *Psychological Review 61:* (1954) 1–4.

logical rather than logical variables of a phenomenon. Finally, as a
psychologist, he strives to continue the tradition of William James.
As America's greatest psychologist, James was an unpretentious
thinker, scientist, philosopher, and humanist; nothing about human
nature, experience, or behavior was unworthy of investigation.

We suspect that MacLeod came to psychology and stayed with it
because the study of man's experiences and behaviors abounds with
unexplored, unsolved, and discarded problems which invite unending
challenges to curiosity in the framework of scholarly exploration. He
accepts that challenge for himself, and arouses us, via *The Persistent
Problems,* to pursue its promise. The promise is what psychology
might become.

The fabric of Professor MacLeod's thinking is the proper context
for *The Persistent Problems.* We will trace that fabric by saying (1)
what his professional *goals* are, (2) what *assumptions* he makes about
what psychology is and how its problems should be studied—guided
by a phenomenological orientation, and (3) what *aims* he believes
psychologists should pursue.

(1) What are Professor MacLeod's professional goals? He quietly
hopes to stir our curiosity about every phenomenon of human
experience and behavior; to promote open and unafraid looking at
the facts; to encourage asking questions about our presuppositions,
methods, and constructs; to foster a more fully life-oriented study of
man at his best; to invite broadening the perspective for the study of
man so as to include facts of experience still refractory to investigation; and to advance the growth of the individual as a person by
means of self-directed use of these habits of thought and action.

(2) What are MacLeod's assumptions about what psychology is
and how its problems should be studied? Psychology is man's continued and disciplined attempt to understand himself in all his complexity. The history of psychological science is the formulation and
progressive reformulation of questions about the persistent problems
which confront us as thinkers and as people. Some of the problems
concerning human nature come from practical life, but most of them
emerge from philosophy. They are, for example, the presumed differences between mind and body (matter), inherited from metaphysics;
the riddle of the basis of knowledge or the nature and validity of
cognitive processes, derived from epistemology; the basis of aesthetic
judgment, taken from aesthetics; the foundation of individual con-

duct, or the question of human motivation, traceable to ethics; finally, the puzzle of the basis of social conduct, nascent in politics. MacLeod argues that these problems contain the beginning questions of human nature.

How, then, should we proceed to study these reformulated problems? Initially, by means of *psychological phenomenology,* says MacLeod. This is so, because it is his *modus operandi;* it forms his matrix of assumptions about what psychology is and what it can become. It is his recommended way of doing psychology.[4]

The phenomenologist begins his inquiry by looking at data—at the facts of immediate human experience untouched by what one *pre-supposes* they mean or by how one assumes they should be classified. Facts of observation (data) are the fountainhead of meaningful distinctions, puzzles, and questions which give rise to psychology's problems. For example, each directly perceived difference between a sentient, acting creature and a rock is a datum which gives rise to a puzzle about two basically separate realities—to a potential dualism of mind and matter; this puzzle, in its many forms, has engaged the curiosity and ingenuity of countless people.

We see then that the facts of experience and observation are influential in imparting direction to the study of man. Data point to, and occasionally map out, problems for investigation. The psychological phenomenologist values facts of observation because they are an ever fertile source of approaching a solution, seeing an old puzzle in a novel way, restating a problem seemingly insoluble in its original form, or suggesting new methods for further study. Problems, in turn, suggest data appropriate to their solution. In reading this book it is profitable to frequently stop and ask: What personal experience, what fact of observation, is related to, or points to, e.g., "my being

4. A more complete discussion of MacLeod's psychological phenomenology as an approach to problems in empirical science may be found in:

MacLeod, R.B., "Phenomenology: a challenge to experimental psychology." In: *Behaviorism and Phenomenology,* T.W. Wann (Ed.). (Chicago: University of Chicago Press, 1964), pp. 47–78.

MacLeod, R.B., "Psychological phenomenology: a propaedeutic to a scientific psychology." In: *Toward Unification in Psychology,* J. R. Royce (Ed.). (Toronto: University of Toronto Press, 1970), pp. 246–266.

Dolezal, H.F., "In honor of Robert Brodie MacLeod: psychological phenomenology face to face with the persistent problems of psychology." *Journal of the History of the Behavioral Sciences, In Press.*

one with the rock?" or, What need I look at, or listen for, in order to help clarify one of the persistent puzzles? Clearly, if we let meaningful and significant experiences and observations guide us in selecting our problems for study, we are more likely to achieve a people-relevant psychology responsive to pressing and value-suffused concerns.

Why should we deny the factual status of meaningful experiences (phenomena) if the issues they point to prove methodologically or conceptually thorny? Why should we discard, for example, as unworthy of study the problems of aesthetic judgment, of the self, and of human devotion and friendship if we find that their quantification is considered impossible if not meaningless? Why should we sacrifice anything to methodological elegance? MacLeod cautions: "Far better a groping, admittedly inadequate investigation of something important than a neat, precise study of something inconsequential."[5] He is committed to the belief that what is essential about a science is neither its particular techniques of investigation nor the degree of precision with which it measures, but the significance of the problems it attempts to solve.

As a method psychological phenomenology is radical in the way it collects, treats, and interprets facts; its practitioner attempts to suspend all theory-derived assumptions in order to observe, describe, and analyze with naiveté and without bias the essential attributes and structures of the facts of direct human experience and behavior.

An example may help. Virtually everyone occasionally reports a seeming "reliving" of a prior experience: we "hear" someone admonishing us, we "see" the face of our beloved, we experience the serenity of a past walk in the forest, we "feel" the joy of a former celebration. The phenomenologist does not jump to label and classify phenomena. Nothing significant is added or explained; our understanding is not enriched by simply attaching labels such as "visual memory," "imagination," or "thinking" to the experience of "seeing" the face of our beloved in his absence. To label usually means to stop looking, describing, and thinking. To further our knowledge we need to know, perhaps, what *structures* (i.e., what identifiable entities of the phenomenal world) are appropriately descriptive; we can

---

5. R. B. MacLeod, "New psychologies of yesterday and today." *Canadian Journal of Psychology 3:* (1949) 211.

ask, for example, what sort of event is "seeing" the face? We need to know what *phenomenal properties of structures* (i.e., what modes or attributes of appearance) characterize the experience; for example, can seeing the face be talked about in terms of its vividness, relative stability, or duration? We further need to know what the *dynamic relations* are between the self and other structures of the field (world) before, during, and after the occurrence; for example, are we reminded of our beloved because of loneliness, hurt, jealousy, celebration? Finally, we need to know along what sorts of *phenomenal dimensions* such an experience might be ordered; for example, what feature of "seeing" the face is similar to or dissimilar from looking at the loved one's face in our presence? What is the reality-irreality status of seeing the face? How is seeing the face described along a subjectivity-objectivity dimension? What sort of relative hedonic pleasantness-unpleasantness is associated with seeing versus looking directly? How does one rate the relative stability-instability of the two observations?

Answers to such open-ended questions may yield some useful data for understanding the nature of experiences that would be foreclosed by mere classification. Hence, the phenomenologist seeks to suspend, or at least to make explicit, the criteria on the basis of which we distinguish such traditional categories as sensation and perception, memory and imagination, thought and emotion, and so on. The point of "bracketing" or suspending assumptions about the nature of an observed phenomenon is to regard facts as they are, not as they are construed. Let experience dictate descriptive categories. Sensibly, MacLeod argues that, as a method, psychological phenomenology is propaedeutic to, even a necessary precursor of, a science of psychology.[6,7] As a preliminary tool it enriches and emancipates our field.

(3) Professor MacLeod's ideas and the approach he sponsors remind us of what psychology can become if we do not lose sight of what is of lasting importance and have the guts to pursue it. The aims of our Psychology are deceptively simple. Get the unmutilated facts and then try to make sense out of them. The facts of human experience may be had by *looking*, in its myriad forms. We strive to

---

6. R. B. MacLeod, "Perceptual constancy and the problem of motivation. *Canadian Journal of Psychology,* 1949, *3*, 64.
7. R. B. MacLeod, "Psychological phenomenology: a propraedeutic to a scientific psychology." In: *Toward Unification in Psychology,* J. R. Royce (Ed.). (Toronto: University of Toronto Press, 1970), p. 260.

attain a cognitive and rational understanding of that which is available for apprehension. We have several tools: we set and define fact-based problems, we generate questions and with them point to possible answers, and we keep a constant check on the justification of our assumptions, the adequacy of our methods, and the correctness of our thinking.[8] Psychology, thus conceived, represents a "fundamental challenge to the traditional scientific conception of man and his relation to the world."[9]

COMMENTARY: CHALLENGE TO DOGMA

What sort of book are we about to read? What is its meaning? An answer it is not: It is a record of the history and systems of Psychology. A better answer is: The meaning of this book points to a challenge. *The Persistent Problems of Psychology* challenges all thinkers.

What is this challenge? There are several, but the main one endangers us if we embrace it, because it demands that we be unceasing questioners of and tolerant dissenters from any powerful and authoritative dogma. We are required to be wary of any pronouncement which prescribes the nature of man, rules what facts are acceptable within an explanation, ordains what methods of study are adequate, and dictates what theoretical constructs and models are an appropriate characterization of the meaning of the facts.

How does one call dogma into question? We will argue that MacLeod's challenge to dogma is composed of six dominant and complexly interwoven themes: They may be conceived as the main structural pillars of *The Persistent Problems,* and they suggest one way of reading the book and thinking about it. We will be concerned with 1) the *origin* of psychological inquiry, 2) its *foundations,* 3) the *processes* of inquiry that permit its continuing development, 4) the *methods* for its maintenance, 5) the *content* from which inquiry derives direction and meaning, and, finally, 6) the *framework* for understanding the methods and content of psychological probing.

(1) What is the origin of psychological inquiry and in what way is

---

8. R. B. MacLeod, "The place of phenomenological analysis in social psychological theory." In: *Social Psychology at the Crossroads.* The University of Oklahoma Lectures in Social Psychology, J. H. Rohrer and M. Sherif (Eds.). (New York: Harper, 1951), p. 238.

9. R. B. MacLeod, "Newtonian and Darwinian conceptions of man; and some alternatives." *Journal of the History of Behavioral Science 6:* (1970) p. 215.

it emphasized? The book does not begin with an abstraction, a great name, or a major epoch. It begins where a phenomenologist would begin, with puzzlement and curiosity, two pervasive phenomena. The book argues that at the root of any exploration is realization of perplexity and seeking for solution. The motivating force behind discovery is shown to be personal participation in puzzlement and the subsequent arousal and exercise of curiosity. We witness how mystery begets and how curiosity maintains exploration. We are led to discover part of the tissue of knowing—the course of its initiation and maintenance.

The process of discovery is illuminated for us in two ways. First, we come to see that psychology is rooted in history; and secondly, with this knowledge, we can see clearly the origin of man's inquiry. Psychology is part of philosophy because self-understanding is an ancient quest; it is part of practical life because it depends on everyday observations; finally, psychology is science "in the making" if we accept the thesis that the essence of our science is unbridled "curiosity harnessed and rendered productive by discipline."[10] Mystery and curiosity function as the connecting links between psychology as history, as philosophy, as practical life, and as burgeoning science.

There is a second way in which the study of the origin of inquiry makes the process of discovery more intelligible. The reader, knowing his history, achieves clarity about how the problems selected for study came into existence, what kind of puzzles gave them birth, and what motivated their pursuit. Mystery and curiosity become two great flywheels of looking, wondering, and theorizing about phenomena. No dogma remains dissent-proof in their continued presence.

(2) What is the foundation of psychological inquiry and what is its role in illuminating modern issues? The book proposes and elucidates two theses. First, the persistent problems of psychology are initially the problems of philosophy.[11] Second, understanding them depends on understanding their development in relation to the broader concerns of philosophers.[12]

---

10. R. B. MacLeod, "The teaching of psychology and the psychology we teach." *American Psychologist 20*: (1965) 349.
11. N. B., If we accept this thesis the *Persistent Problems* is an introduction to the field of psychology, not merely to its history.
12. R. B. MacLeod, *The Persistent Problems of Psychology,* Chapter 1 (Pittsburgh: Duquesne University Press, 1975), pp. 31ff.

The first thesis is persuasively argued. On reading the book we learn that it is quite difficult to ask a question or to formulate a problem whose foundation is not clearly in one or more of the ancestral philosophical areas. For example, modern questions about the complex relationship between perception, thought, and motor performance are recognized to be solidly rooted in the mind-body dispute (metaphysics); or, current experiments in cognition, say, probing the relationship between inborn (genetic) and environmental contributions in the genesis of environment ("space") perception are revealed as an outgrowth of epistemology. Virtually all questions asked may be viewed as a steadfast savoring—directly or indirectly—of the outstanding riddles of philosophy. While some of these questions have been dodged, dissolved or judged, in principle, to be unanswerable, many of the intents and meanings behind these broader issues will undoubtedly always be with us in one guise or another.

The second thesis is equally well sustained. The continued understanding of psychology's problems is to be sought in their development in philosophy; indeed, throughout much of the book we discover that by losing sight of the initial issues we run the danger of stripping both our problem and our observation of significance. However, maintaining an historical perspective with respect to philosophical concerns is not the only basis for understanding psychology's issues. In reading *The Persistent Problems,* one of the most engaging activities for the reader may be called "mosaic-watching" and "mosaic-constructing". We see an historical view of man in many contexts. We witness the rich cross-fertilization of etymology, art, literature, religion, politics, and economics with understanding of human experience as the beneficiary. For example, extensive dissections of the human body made by Leonardo and Michelangelo (also revealed later in the sketches of Vesalius) led to discoveries that challenged the dogma of Galen and the authority of the Church.[13] It is refreshing to encounter a well-documented argument which emphasizes the heuristic of historical continuity.

(3) What are the processes that permit the continuing development of psychological inquiry? The myth of the slow, steady, unidirectional accumulation of knowledge may be just that—a myth.

---

13. R. B. MacLeod, *The Persistent Problems of Psychology,* Chapter 3. (Pittsburgh: Duquesne University Press, 1975), p. 100.

This book affords inspection of another thesis. Growth and advancement in science proceed by means of reformulation of questions and issues. Inquiry develops via the progressive differentiation, refinement, and reformulation of the persistent problems.

The book establishes a credible link between the origin, foundation, and processes of inquiry. In this chain, perplexity is the first step toward enlightenment. The reader learns how, in the hands of psychologists, every major philosophical question has undergone conversion, transformation, and refinement.

How these puzzles of philosophy become empirically testable propositions is the main, recurrent theme of *The Persistent Problems.* It is a story-line with several sub-plots revealing that the reformulation of questions is anything but orderly and narrowly pathbound. Yet it is possible to differentiate some of the constituent parts (principles) of this process. MacLeod does not formally identify these principles; hence, not until we name them for ourselves do we realize that Socratic midwifery has been at work again.

Two principles deserve commentary, particularly since they are conceptual tools *par excellence* in questioning dogma: first, the articulation of implicitly held assumptions; second, the challenge of those presuppositions. The first principle asserts that discovery is frequently preceded by detecting and expressing the unspoken presuppositions that underlie a method of gathering data, a particular way of casting a problem, a model of explanation, or a doctrine of thought. The second one asserts, and the book amply demonstrates (especially Chapter 3), that major advances recorded in the history of western science were in each instance prefaced by contesting existing assumptions.[14,15]

These, then, are the means whereby rigid belief is ruffled, blind tradition revised, prized dictum recalled, cherished dogma uprooted, and accepted authority confronted with constructive irreverence. (The hardest task is to entertain the thought that some of these rigid

14. R. B. MacLeod, "Newtonian and Darwinian conceptions of man; and some alternatives." *Journal of the History of the Behavioral Sciences 6:* (1970) 208.

15. A careful reading reveals that the author identifies and impugns, among others, assumptions underlying the Newtonian model of causation as sufficient for a meaningful account of human motivated conduct. For more details consult:
R. B. MacLeod, "Newtonian and Darwinian conceptions of man; and some alternatives." 207–218.
R. B. MacLeod, "Teleogy and theory of human behavior." *Science 125:* (1957) 477–480.

beliefs are our own; next in difficulty is leveling these principles at our own pre-judgments and prejudices.)

One can learn from the book how formidable thinkers have phrased their questions and why they chose the form they did. Subtle or not, this is part of the MacLeod nudge, his invitation and encouragement to carry the burden and enjoy the rewards of framing our own questions and answers.

(4) What are the methods that help maintain psychological inquiry? The book has little to say about ways to perpetuate or augment the methodological *status quo* of scientific investigation although it acknowledges its standard procedures—observation, classification, formulating and testing hypotheses, induction, deduction, generalization, and so on. Rather, its emphasis is on elucidating the role of phenomenology as a preliminary tool in the scientific study of man.

Every method of observation is dependent on its user and interferes with the object of observation—with the very process we set out to measure. Therefore, the question arises: Is psychology—man studying himself—even practicable? Perhaps we are in danger of being disqualified by our very own Heisenbergian principle of uncertainty (indeterminacy). The dilemma is this: how do we make sure that the phenomena we observe and want to examine are not biased or distorted by observation itself? The phenomenological method is designed to grapple with this dilemma. It calls for monitoring the assumptions and biases of observation and analysis. "Nobody contends that you can ever place in brackets all your biases. But you can at least become aware and you can at least deliberately shift from one bias to another bias to another bias and get successive perspectives on the phenomena that you're dealing with."[16] Here, the uniqueness of the book is that it begins with and achieves a phenomenological orientation. Both the book and the orientation commence from the point of view of a naive observer; both beckon the reader to make full use of the validity afforded him by his wholesome naivete.

(5) What is the content from which psychological inquiry derives direction and meaning? The content of conscious experience is the common spring which supplies us with the materials for further

---

16. R. B. MacLeod, "Concluding remarks." In: *The MacLeod Symposium*, D. Krech (Ed.). (Ithaca, New York: Cornell University, Department of Psychology, 1973), pp. 119–120.

observation, description, deduction, induction, generalization, and with ideas for analysis and synthesis. We are already acquainted with the five classes of problems which make up the framework of specific investigation. They include the general topics of artistic and scientific knowledge, of morality, of human sensibility, and of the processes and the products of understanding in all its aspects. A more immediate object of inquiry, however, is man's experience of himself.

Part of the texture of conscious experience is the phenomenon of *self,* the recognition of *linguistic* and other forms of *communication,* and the knowledge of meanings or *value-properties* which are experienced as inhering in our actions, in the actions of others, and in the events of the perceived world at large. To make sense of the content of inquiry requires thinking about how these phenomena interface with the persistent problems. As we read the book (especially Chapters 2, 4, 6, and 7), discussion of these phenomena slips in and out of focus.

The self as a phenomenal structure continues to be resistant to countless attempts to sweep it under the rug of linguistic analysis or physical reductionism. A singular or plural first person pronoun has made its appearance in every known language; certainly, the self as given in experience deserves a firm place in our study. The self also becomes a vital concept in the study of consciousness; it is the silent anchor of aesthetic judgment, of perception, and of all other forms of cognition; it is the center for freedom and servitude; it is a system within the complex field of social conduct; finally, the self is a percept as well as an agent in communication. Any study of human motivation, any discussion of causation, of intentionality, or of free will and determinism may gain validity by including the phenomenal self.

The myriad processes of communicating and gaining meanings linguistically represent key aspects of experience which cannot be arbitrarily isolated and ignored when considering any of the persistent problems. What an intriguing set of puzzles they suggest! On the one hand, "we could not use symbols consistently if there were not differences in experience to which they refer":[17] the wisdom of

---

17. R. B. MacLeod, "Phenomenology and cross-cultural research." In: *Interdisciplinary Relationship in the Social Sciences,* M. Sherif and C. Sherif (Eds.). (Chicago: Aldine, 1969), p. 183.

common language has enshrined countless perceptual differentia-
tions. On the other hand, language imposes categories on our description of experience which may be inappropriate to the facts; the
danger is in mistaking a linguistic stereotype for a description of
what is genuinely *there for the self* as a cognitive structure.

The fact of value crisscrosses every problem. It has a long and
honored history. Values appear to be the property of objective
structure; analogous to objective properties of things and events,
they are perceptually available. *Value-orientations* may be cognitive
or motivational structures and become part of the framework within
which conduct is regulated and judged.[18] It is unclear how any
theory of human motivation can ignore this phenomenon and claim
fidelity to fact.

Charting the interminable connections and significant relations
among the facts of self, causation, communication, and value properties and, in turn, relating these relations to their appropriate problems is a never-ending task which we inherit as thoughtful students of
psychology.

(6) What is the framework for understanding the method and
content of psychological inquiry? The shape of knowledge derives
from the problems thinkers seek to solve, the empirical foundation
they manage to establish, and the resultant organizing and explanatory framework they produce. Both our solution to practical puzzles
and our approach to theoretical issues entail a theory of man.

Organizing principles, assumptions, beliefs, and values guide us
when we classify a fact, phrase a question, or formulate a problem. A
given point of view may range from being quite fragmented, contra-
dictory, and poorly articulated to forming a highly structured system
of interpretation. Such a well-formulated, self-consistent interpretation is known as a "doctrine."

MacLeod presents us with a seemingly interminable stream of
questions, part-answers, and further questions, and the processes of
inquiry—differentiation and reformulation—eventually generate a
form which these questions and their implied answers take. One
might imagine that both the import of the questions and the intent
of the answers yielded could take innumerable forms; yet this is not

---

18. R. B. MacLeod, *Religious Perspectives of College Teaching* (New Haven: Edward W.
    Hazen Foundation, 1952), p. 19.

so. Only a handful of essentially different interpretations evolved when the philosophers of Greece sought to answer the perennial questions. Their doctrines are so basic that they are very much a part of our own thinking, though we may not be able to name them or identify the matrix of assumptions which underlies each. The book distinguishes five classical doctrines of man. They are relativism, as pronounced by Protagoras, materialism as conceived by Democritus, idealism as defended by Plato, Aristotle's teleology, and the religious doctrine of man. Some of these interpretations or systems of understanding address a single persistent problem, others provide a means of evaluating them all.

How are we to assess the self-consistency of a given thesis or the relative effectiveness of two competing theses? We are meant to evaluate for ourselves, of course; accordingly, early in Chapter 2 we are furnished a set of tools, a schema, with which we may examine critically not only the ancient doctrines of man, but any system of structuring knowledge. Four key questions make up this schema. We want to know of any doctrine or theory: What problem is being solved? What data are accepted as appropriate to its solution? What methods of data selection are proposed as effective in solving it? Finally, what constructs of explanation are dictated by the data, method, and problem? Answers to these questions enable us to discover and judge what a doctrine or theory asserts and what it assumes; whether it explains all it purports to explain, and whether another contender is strictly comparable or not.

The classical doctrines of man articulate the significant puzzles and solutions that are part of the fabric of every generation of thoughtful people. They absorb questions and foreshadow answers with a simplicity that either astounds or exasperates. Either way, they are still with us. Both the subject matter and the manner of presentation make *The Persistent Problems* dateless.

FUTURE DIRECTION: BACK TO WILLIAM JAMES

MacLeod, true to MacLeod, gives us a start, and only a start, In fact, he gives us less than even he intended because the book is incomplete; yet, if we are right about the importance of what he is doing, only a single significant chapter is missing. If he could have

written just one more of the chapters he planned, it would have been
the one on James' restatement of the persistent problems. He actively taught James in his graduate seminars and recently edited one
symposium publication in his honor.[19] It seems to us that he was
preparing to write the chapter. However, lest the reader be too
disappointed, MacLeod would be the first to insist that the loss is not
as great as it might seem. He would point us toward a library shelf,
better yet, to a paperback bookstore, and suggest that we read and
reread a copy of James' *Principles of Psychology.* Here is why:
"James' *Principles* is without question the most literate, the most
provocative, and at the same time the most intelligible book on
psychology that has ever appeared in English or in any other language."[20] If we can be enticed to accept MacLeod's invitation we
will be doing what he loved best: reading the original source.

Like James, Professor MacLeod prefers not to be identified as
either moving forward and onward with the *Zeitgeist* or being one of
its movers. All the noise created by and associated with the supposed
march of Science *qua* Science is anathema to him; yet, in retrospect,
he may emerge among modern psychologists as a leading contributor
to a renewed awareness. It is the awareness that both our most
prevalent conceptions of man and approaches to the study of man
have become too narrow and constrictive; it is the awareness that our
psychology is too intolerant of asking or being asked difficult and
down to earth questions about people as they are, when these
questions do not conform to traditional boundaries; it is the awareness that our psychology is ashamed of tentative probing of "disrepu-
table" phenomena; and it is the awareness that our psychology is
often too hurried to welcome investigations too broad to be manage-
able in one fell swoop.

This is the book of a thinker, gentle yet rebellious. It is the last,
loving gift of a man uncompromising in his search for sense and
excellence. He is unconcerned with fashion and unsettling because he
shields, under the umbrella of perpetual curiosity, anyone's free
investigation and expression of unpopular ideas. The book is the

---

19. *William James: Unfinished Business,* Ed. R. B. MacLeod. (Washington, D.C.: Ameri-
    can Psychological Association, 1969).
20. ibid, p. iii.

unfinished seeking of a man patient in his quest for good questions and answers, tolerant of uncertainty, and temperate in his expectation for reaching final conclusions.

Hubert Dolezal
Massachusetts Institute of Technology

Thomas Toleno
Marlboro College

September 1974

PART I

The Classical Period

I

The Awakening
of
Psychological Curiosity

THE SCIENTIFIC ATTITUDE

"WONDER," said Socrates to Theaetetus, "is the feeling of a philosopher, and philosophy begins in wonder." Through the mouth of Socrates Plato was expressing his belief that in humble curiosity about the nature of things is to be found the beginning of wisdom. Philosophy in Plato's language included what we now mean by science. To be a scientist, or a philosopher, is to be persistently and humbly curious, to be constantly inquiring but to be willing to check one's observations in every possible way by the most reliable methods of verification. Science, as we conceive it, is humble and disciplined curiosity.

To be curious is natural. The lower animals spontaneously explore the unknown. The toddling child cannot pass a hedgehog's hole without investigating it. The elderly gossip listens eagerly on the party line for news about her neighbors. These are examples of curiosity, but not necessarily of humble and disciplined curiosity. To be disciplined is to question every observation until it is verified. To be humble is to realize that any observation may be incomplete, that any generalization may be superseded. To be a scientist is to be willing to live in a world of probabilities, to question one's present hypotheses when one is confronted by a new fact, to search the world for more facts that may confirm or negate one's hypotheses.

The true scientist observes, questions, tests, observes again, tests again, and then raises further questions; he proceeds slowly towards

17

certainty. He usually begins with a problem, which may be practical or theoretical. In solving it he discovers that he has revealed some further problems, which he then proceeds to investigate. Sometimes he arrives at certainty; but usually he does not. It may be that the story of science is in essence the story of the progressive reformulation of problems.

This, at any rate is the story of psychology. Since the beginning of recorded thought man has wondered about the nature of himself and about his relation to the world about him; and we find evidences of this kind of curiosity in the nonliterate cultures of today. Man has wondered about the differences between living and nonliving things, about the differences between animals and men, and about the differences between some people and other people; and, beyond all these, about the uniqueness of man himself. Down through the centuries these problems have been stated in varying ways, their specific formulations always colored by the spirit of the times, some problems accented and others obscured. As the methods of observation and verification have improved, some of the persistent problems of psychology have become more clearly and tightly formulated; but none has been finally solved, and some have tended to slip out of focus. An historical perspective may help us to appreciate, not merely the progress we have made, but also the gaps in our present understanding and the challenges to further inquiry.

What makes man begin to wonder about his own nature? About the historical origins of psychological curiosity we can only speculate, since there are no written records. It would seem plausible, however, that there have always been two kinds of instigation. (1) The practical problems of everyday living, when seriously considered, lead beyond themselves to the broader problems of human nature and invite a search for fundamental principles. (2) The broad problems of philosophy and science require for their solution a detailed scrutiny of the facts of experience and behavior. Let us take a glance at each type of challenge.

THE CHALLENGE FROM EVERYDAY LIVING

The student of psychology may find his first interest stimulated by problems that immediately confront him. He may be an undergraduate who wishes he could study more efficiently, a parent who is puzzled by the behavior of his children, a businessman who would like to "apply psychology" in his dealings with people, or a politician who thinks that "psychology" may help him to sway his audiences or "size up" his opponents. Most of the practical problems of everyday living have to do directly or indirectly with people, and we have rightly come to the conclusion that the person who knows "why people do what they do" has a great advantage. We cannot quarrel with the statement that "to be a good salesman you have to be a good psychologist," for the good salesman has learned to observe without prejudice and to invest his own chances of success in the soundness of his judgment. Psychology is thus an eminently practical subject.

We must, however, take a much broader view of the challenge of practical living to psychological curiosity. The salesman or politician or parent, albeit genuinely curious about the why's and wherefore's of human behavior, is likely to rest content with a few dependable rules of thumb that will enable him to meet his immediate problems. Seldom is he led beyond these to wonder about the nature of man and about man's place in the world. It is the larger problems of living that provide the real challenge. When the individual, while wrestling with his own personal problems, can see these as merely instances of problems that are universal he is well on his way to becoming a scientist.

The history of the other sciences is studded with examples of practical concerns that give rise to genuine scientific curiosity. For thousands of years the flatlands of the Nile Delta have been dependent on irrigation rather than on rainfall, a practical context in which an interest in geometry and hydraulics could be nourished. Early navigators steered their ships by the stars, and the science of astronomy was born. The laws of falling bodies, and eventually the laws of gravitation, owed much for their formulation to man's desire to bombard his enemies with projectiles. The needs of medical practice, of animal husbandry, of agriculture, and even of horse racing have unleashed man's curiosity about the nature of plant and animal life. And the most recent and perhaps the most important of all challenges to scientific curiosity came when physical scientists during wartime were mobilized to produce the most powerful bomb that man had ever conceived. Few of the physicists involved are happy about the death and destruction that resulted; what attracted them was the opportunity to unravel more of the secrets of nature.

Curiosity about the nature of man has, as we shall see, a similar history. Little people at all times have been faced with practical human problems and have worked out their rules of thumb. Every once in a while, however, we find a great person—a philosopher or, later, a scientist—who is able to see the general through the particular, who grasps the essence of a human problem and gives it a universal formulation. Such men are Plato, Aristotle, Augustine, Descartes, Locke, Hume, Fechner, Darwin, James, and many others whom we shall discuss. These men were persistently curious about human nature. They had their practical problems to begin with, but they were lured beyond the practical towards the unknown.

Perhaps more urgently than ever before in history, the problems that face mankind today demand solutions based on an understanding of man himself. The finger that presses the key in a "push-button" war is ruled by a human impulse. The lapse of judgment that brings an airplane crashing to destruction is a human failure. The sane proposal that reestablishes cooperation between conflicting groups is a product of human genius. These are practical situations in which the human factor has always been recognized, but until recently it has been regarded as one of the unknown and unpredictable elements in the situation, not as something that might excite the curiosity of the scientist. Let us glance briefly at four practical fields that obviously invite scientific study. These are: (1) inter-group tension, (2) government, (3) technological change, and (4) education.

INTER-GROUP TENSION

One of the most obvious sources of inter-group tension is nationalism. When we think of mankind as a whole we inevitably think in terms of nations. During the past two hundred years virtually all the major wars have been fought between nations. As we contemplate the possibility of an orderly world society we envisage a union of nations. Nationality is thus a social fact that must be reckoned with if we are to think clearly about human problem, and, as such, is psychologically interesting. What really challenges us, however, is not nationality but nationalism. We speak of nationalism when the feeling of membership in a nation has become so charged with emotion that it dominates behavior to the exclusion of other values. Nationalism constitutes an ever-present threat to world peace.

We must note, however, that nationalism has not always repre-sented a threat to peace. In Joan of Arc's day (early fifteenth century) the people of France owed their primary allegiance not to their king but to their feudal lords. Nationalism offered an ideal of unity that gave meaning to the terms "France" and "Frenchman" and eventually eliminated the feudal wars. In the late nineteenth century Bismarck welded a motley array of rival states into a single German nation. In the eighteenth century a common threat and a common aspiration drew together the thirteen states on the Atlantic seaboard, and gradually a nation came into being. We can see the same process at work today, in India, in Indonesia, in North Africa, where a passionate nationalism has marked the emergence of new and broader allegiances. Thus at one stage in the development of soci-eties, while nations are coming into being, nationalism seems to be constructive. At a later stage, as established nations compete with one another for power or for survival, nationalism becomes more and more destructive.

Should we encourage, or should we attempt to suppress, national-istic movements and nationalistic attitudes? Or are there alternative solutions? We cannot here attempt to answer such questions. What is clear, however, is that no satisfactory answer can be found until we know more about the social attitudes of people, how attitudes develop, how attitudes can be changed, what determines a person's allegiances, how people can become unified by a common goal as well as by a common threat. The practical challenge of nationalism is to the development of a psychology of social man.

Another important source of inter-group tension is found in the common tendency to identify people in terms of presumed "racial" heritage. The obvious differences we see in color of skin, texture of hair, shape of skull, conformation of face, and so forth, tempt us to conclude that physically distinguishable human groups spring from originally different stocks, each with its own intrinsic characteristics and some superior to the others. In many parts of the world "racial" groups, because of their supposed inferiority or because they are regarded as a threat, are denied full participation in the life of their society. The most widely publicized examples of racial discrimina-tion today have to do with the position of the Black in the United States and in South Africa, but parallel cases can be found almost everywhere.

Biologists and physical anthropologists are becoming increasingly dissatisfied with the concept of race. There is no clear evidence of separate racial origins, there are no reliable physical indices of racial membership, and the apparent psychological differences seem to be more closely related to climate, nutrition and culture than to inherent biological factors. Nevertheless, "race" is a psychological fact. Regardless of the scientific validity of the concept, people *feel* themselves as belonging to a particular race and perceive others as members of racial groups. It is our feelings and perceptions that regulate our behavior. When we have prejudged a group to be superior or inferior, and then identify an individual as a member of that group, our perception of that individual is likely to be correspondingly distorted. Similarly, our conception of our own race will affect our self-perceptions and our behavior. "Blood will tell" is a familiar theme in nineteenth century literature, and it is a notion that we have not outlived. For many people today the thought of "racial mixture" is utterly abhorrent.

As in the case of nationalism, racialism must not be regarded as without its positive value. Pride in one's own (possibly fictitious) heritage can be a constructive influence; witness the tenacity with which the Jews have sought through the centuries to maintain racial purity and thereby the integrity of the Jewish ideal, and the stabilizing influence of the traditional Chinese identification of the individual with his ancestors. But racialism is more frequently a barrier to peaceful living. Racialism means judging people in categories rather than as individuals and judging them on the basis of supposedly inherited traits rather than on the basis of what they have achieved. "East is East, and West is West, and never the twain shall meet" implies a psychological theory which, if true, would mean that there are inherent and insurmountable racial differences. The sad fact is that the belief in race as a biological reality is still with us. Hitler was able to nourish his movement toward world domination on the myth of Nordic superiority, and the recurrent agitation for "white" supremacy is buttressed by the same kind of myth. Today racialism is a threat to peace, second only to nationalism.

The rivalry between socio-economic classes provides a third source of tension. Social classes are to be found in virtually all societies, although in different societies they may be differently structured. There may, for instance, be a class of nobility, a class of civil servants, a white-collar class, and so forth. In some societies, as in

India, the classes have become so rigid as to justify the term "caste", a social group into which one is born and from which one can seldom move.

The merit of the class system is that it simplifies social living. Members of each class have their own duties and privileges, usually their own class-determined occupations, and often a type of housing, costume, or even speech distinctive of the class. In a stable, class-structured society the individual knows what is expected of him and what is not permitted, even though these may not be written down in law. He may perhaps dream of marrying "above his station" or rising to an occupation of higher status, but the chances of his so doing are very small.

Industrialization and the extension of the frontiers of the western world dealt a shattering blow to the class system. Traditional class lines became increasingly blurred, new occupations emerged, new skills were needed and were rewarded by wealth, and the spread of education awakened countless individuals to the realization that they might be regarded as human beings rather than as mere members of a class. Some theorists even began to play with the idea of a classless society. This has not been achieved, even in the Communist countries, but it is clear that we are moving slowly towards a society in which the accident of birth will have only a minor influence on the career of the individual.

The achievement of liberty carries its own penalty in the form of new problems. One shattered tradition brings other traditions down in ruins. In the industrialized West the new liberty threatened to stratify society in a new way, *viz.*, the Exploited versus the Exploiters, a new class system that was to supersede the old system of multiple classes. There was to be a war between the classes, with the Workers triumphant. This has not taken place. Society has, however, been stratified in new ways. Having challenged the traditions of class, the members of various occupational groups,—for instance, industrial workers, small businessmen, farmers, teachers, medical practitioners—have organized themselves to promote their respective interests. There is no longer the belief that one group is intrinsically more worthy than another; it is a straightforward struggle among equals, a struggle in which their common membership in larger national and world groups is sometimes forgotten.

Conflicts between Labor and Management in big industry provide perhaps the best examples of the practical psychological problems that face us. A few generations ago Labor was merely a commodity; Management wielded the power. Today Labor bargains as an equal with Management. With our new appreciation of the dignity of the individual, and with the common man's growing appreciation of his own dignity, the human problems of industry assume new dimensions. These were simple in the day when the laborer could be treated as a tool; today he must be treated as a human being. The story of the labor movement has many bloody chapters, but it shows how two different interest groups have gradually, with many fumbles, come to some degree of mutual understanding. They have worked out techniques of arbitration, and have had many of these written into law. As we look to the future, however, and as we face each succeeding crisis in industrial relations, we can see clearly that we need more than a set of practical procedures; we need a science of human relations that can be applied wherever human beings with different interests seek a common ground for action.

Examples of inter-group tension could be extended indefinitely. There are, for example, the great ideological differences that seem to be tearing mankind asunder and the smaller political differences that add spice to the life of a nation; there are conflicts among the great religious traditions and conflicts among the denominations of any one religion; there are countless tussles, sometimes quite friendly, among communities, neighborhood groups and families. All such tensions present practical problems that require for their solution an understanding of human nature and skill in human relations. From the biggest to the smallest problems, from the problems of international and interracial relations to the problems of community harmony, all invite an inquiry into the laws that govern human behavior.

GOVERNMENT

Every citizen of a democracy shares responsibility for the government of his country and, if he is farsighted, for the government of the world. He shares it when he abides by the traffic laws, when he casts his vote for a candidate for election, when he protests against a government policy, when he argues politics over the back fence with his neighbor. In a democracy the government is "ours", not "theirs".

We are proud when something fine is accomplished; we are ashamed when our government has fallen short of the ideal. In a modest way each of us makes the decisions that determine the fate of all, and each of us bears the blame if something goes wrong.

The governing of men is thus a practical problem that confronts not only the person who achieves a position of leadership but also the less conspicuous people upon whose support the leader depends. Each little decision—to violate a traffic law, to stay away from the voting booth, to sign a petition—is a political decision in that it affects the lives of other people. Every such decision implies some sort of belief about human behavior. "Even if I drive too fast, I can trust the other fellow to be careful." "Just one vote doesn't make any difference anyway." "My signature on this petition may not do any good, but at least it relieves my conscience." We need not judge these statements as right or wrong, but we must recognize that each involves an assessment of what people are likely to do, *i.e.*, it represents in some measure a psychological judgment.

Every system of government has always implied a psychological theory, ranging from the extreme of autocracy, with its assumption that the common man cannot be trusted to think for himself, to the extreme of democracy, with its assumption that the opinion of any man is equal in value to that of any other man. In Western society we have veered toward the democratic theory, without reaching the extreme. In an autocracy the psychological problem is relatively simple; rule is by the strongest in their own interests or in what they think are the interests of the people. All the autocrats have to know is how to regulate the behavior of people—not easy, but not impossible when they have full control of power. In a democracy the psychological problem is infinitely more complex. People are regarded as free individuals whose opinions must ultimately determine the course of government. Leadership in a democracy depends on persuasion, and persuasion is successful only when the persuader understands not only the needs but also the hopes and fears and prejudices of those he is trying to persuade.

As the world moves towards a democratic form of government, the practical need for psychological understanding becomes increasingly apparent. If government is to be by consent of the governed, and if the decisions of those who govern are to be in accord with the real wishes of the people, we must have a science that explores the motivation and the thinking of people. The legislator who proposes a law, the executive who administers it, and the common man who registers his verdict in the voting booth, must each experience at least a momentary curiosity about the human consequences of his decision. He must at least wonder why anyone could be so bull-headed as to disagree with him; he might even wonder about the basis of his own decision. Release this curiosity from the immediately practical context and we have a scientist who is wondering about the basis of human attitudes, how attitudes can be changed, why we believe what we believe, what factors govern our decisions, how people with different predispositions can communicate with one another.

TECHNOLOGICAL CHANGE

One of the most fascinating chapters in the history of man deals with his continuous readjustment to the new tools that he himself has discovered. The mastery of fire and the invention of the wheel initiated major revolutions in human life, and even apparently minor developments like the printing press and the telescope produced unforeseen changes in man's mode of living. Technological change has always had its human repercussions, but during the past two centuries the pace of the change has accelerated so rapidly as to leave us almost breathless. The combustion engine, the electric light, the telephone, the radio, antibiotics, outer space, nuclear fission and a host of other developments have demanded continuous adjustments and readjustments. We look to next year with the assumption that this year's car and refrigerator will by then be outmoded, and we look back to the horse-and-buggy days as though they belonged to prehistory. The expectation of continuous technological change has become an integral part of the outlook of the western world.

In other parts of the world, however, the new technology has come as a shock. In Africa, in India, and even in China, the new machines have upset the old order of living. Not only do the machines demand new skills, for which there may be no adequate training facilities, but new avenues of communication have opened up a strange world of ideas that are quite at variance with tradition. The West has lived through its industrial revolution gradually, albeit with some major maladjustments. In the non-Western world the impact of technology has been thoroughly disrupting, breaking down ancient ways of living and time-honored ways of thinking. Small wonder that some of the non-Western nations seem at times to be behaving in an irrational way!

The common man faces the problem of technological change when his wife buys a new food mixer or when his children demand a television set. He may become mildly curious about the relation between his enriched nutrition and his feeling of well-being or about the effect of western thrillers on adolescent attitudes. If he is scientifically minded, however, his curiosity will lead him much further. He will begin to wonder about the broad relations between nutrition and mentality, about the influences that steer a person in his development. Eventually he will begin to wonder about a big question: What is technology doing to human beings? And this will lead him to ask more specific questions: What is happening to technologically underdeveloped people who have suddenly come under the influence of Western methods? Can they compete success-fully with the West? If not, is their failure due to cultural tradition? to climate? to nutrition? Or, have they a way of life that is really worth preserving? In what ways have automobiles, movies and radio shaped the development of people? And what will happen to people as technology harnesses new sources of power, solves the problem of prolonging life, smooths the process of communication until any one person can become completely present to any other person anywhere else in the world?

The effects of technological change, when we think of them, stagger the imagination. Modern technology represents a growing mastery by humans of the resources of the natural world. The thinking man must wonder whether our understanding of ourselves is sufficient to enable us to cope with all the changes that are to come. He must wonder about human limitations, about human capacities for growth and adjustment, about the processes whereby humans become creative.

EDUCATION

Perhaps no practical setting includes more psychological problems than does that of education, not merely the formal setting of the classroom but the process of mastering skills and acquiring knowledge that goes on throughout life. In earliest infancy the individual begins to be molded into a pattern that will become his characteristic personality, a pattern that will become more stable as he grows older but that will always be capable of some change. Parents watch with fascination the growth of motor coordination and the extension of vocabulary, worry about the rights and wrongs of corporal punishment, and fumblingly try to help with the homework. Whether they realize it or not, they are dealing with psychological problems and are operating on the basis of psychological principles. The thoughtful parent wonders not merely whether he ought or ought not to punish his child for telling lies but what has really motivated the child to lie, what the child's conception of truth is, what the effect of punishment is on the child's attitudes. As he continues to observe he may begin to realize that the child is living in a strange and fascinating world, in many ways quite different from that of the adult, a world that would be interesting to recapture and to explore.

For the teacher the psychological problems are even more insistent. Every teacher knows that there are no two children who are exactly the same, in ability, in temperament, or in attitudes. There are gifted children, lethargic children, children who respond to praise by working harder and children whose response is a slackening of effort. Her task is to present her lessons in such a way that each child will find them interesting and will be able to master them. For this she must understand not only her subject but also her pupils. Many an apparently competent teacher seems to succeed merely by using the "tricks of the trade," by maintaining discipline, distributing regular rewards and punishments, systematically reviewing important lessons, and so forth, without necessarily understanding the psychological principles that underlie the practice. The really good teacher, however, finds herself becoming interested in the psychological problems of individual differences, of learning, of motivation and personality formation. It is a hopeful sign that the training of every teacher is now designed to alert her to the psychological problems of her profession.

To the pupil himself—and this means not merely the school child or the university student but also every adult who is trying to master something new—the process of learning can be a source of psychological interest. Learning to operate a new machine or to speak a new language or to play a new game is in itself a fascinating experience in that it makes us wonder about the complex of factors that enter into the learning process. It has been said that no psychologist should ever be bored because the very experience of being bored should be sufficiently interesting to relieve his boredom.

Educational theory, like political theory, always involves a theory of man. During the past hundred years, and particularly during the past half-century, the practical problems of education have provided much of the stimulus to psychological inquiry. The modern revolution in educational practice began with the realization that children must be thought of not as miniature adults but as people of a different kind whose mental processes must be understood if we are to cope with them. As we shall see later, the interest in child development was linked to the broad problem of human development as such. Today we have an unprecedented interest in developmental psychology. Parents are eager to know how to rear their children. Should they wield the authoritarian whip? Should they allow the children to steer their own course? Teachers are worrying about what they are doing, and what they should do, to the developing individuals entrusted to them. And all of us are concerned about our own growth and development. We want to become better, happier, more effective people. How do we go about it?

The practical problems of everyday living seem to call especially for a science of *social* man; and this is quite intelligible, since so many of the situations that provoke us to psychological thought involve our relations with other people. Indeed, the characteristic emphasis of today's psychology is social. We are interested in the behavior of groups, in the nature of socialization, in the development of the person within a social context, in the ways in which the individual perceives and reacts to other people. When we view man's practical problems in historical perspective, however, we realize that it was not always the social problem that aroused his greatest curiosity. For many centuries man's practical problems were as likely to be set in a religious as in a social context. Only a short time ago the question "What can I believe?" was still intensely practical; the answer might mean the difference between salvation and eternal damnation. The present century may seem to have robbed it of some of its urgency, but it is still a question that challenges us to examine the psychological basis of knowledge. As we review the development of psychological theory we shall see that practical and theoretical interests can never be kept completely separate.

PRIMITIVE DUALISM

When we attempt to determine the origin of psychological curiosity we can do little more than speculate. There is an interesting lead, however, that comes from etymology. The Greek word *psuche* originally meant "breath", as did its Latin counterpart *anima*. It seems plausible to assume that the subsequent concepts of "soul," "spirit" and "mind" were derived from the concept of breath. The most striking change that takes place in a body at the moment of death is that it ceases to breathe; hence one might conclude that there is something uniquely important about breath. According to the Biblical account, God formed man from the dust of the earth and "breathed into his nostrils the breath of life". Breath is invisible and intangible, yet essential to living. What, our early ancestors may have asked, is the nature of this mysterious something?

Whether or not this speculation is sound, we cannot fail to be impressed by the frequency with which we encounter a distinction between the two kinds of reality: (1) a reality that is thing-like, inert and resistant, like rocks and blocks of wood, incapable of spontaneous action, and (2) a reality that is not thing-like, that feels and chooses and manipulates things. This is the primitive dualism of mind and matter that has taken so many forms in the history of human thought. It may be that this distinction does not exist on the simplest levels of psychological organization, in animals, in early infancy, possibly in the thinking of the most "primitive" people; but there is ample evidence to suggest that it becomes clearer as the psychological world of the individual becomes more richly articulated. We may not assume that the universality of the dualism means that its content is everywhere the same. The child early makes the distinction between Me and Not-Me, and this is a dualism, but this is far from a sophisticated dualism of Mind and Matter. It is not even a dualism of Animate and Inanimate, for it would appear that many of the things that we adults regard as inanimate are for the child alive and sensitive. Similarly, in many cultures widely different from our own, it is generally believed that such objects as rocks, trees and mountains may be inhabited by spirits, a type of belief that is sometimes labeled Animistic. This, too, is a dualism of two kinds of reality, but not necessarily the dualism present in the world of the child.

Thus, when we assert that a primitive dualism is a natural, possibly an inevitable, way of apprehending the world when one begins to think about it, we must guard against the danger of reading false meanings into it. The important thing to note is that psychological speculation has traditionally begun with the attempt to find the relationship between what seems to be two quite different kinds of reality. These have sometimes been thought of simply as things that are alive and things that are not alive, or as bodies that can think and bodies that cannot think, although usually the distinctions have been much subtler. At any rate, in the early history of psychology the word "soul" (Greek *psuche*, Latin *anima*) came to represent the essence of the problem. The word acquired many different meanings, and it was eventually dropped from the vocabulary of psychology because of its theological connotations, but the problem persisted. Stated in very general terms, the problem is: What is the nature of this reality that seems to differentiate man from the animals and from non-living things? Is it an entity, or a capacity, or a property? Can it exist by itself? Does it act in accordance with the laws of physical nature, or does it conform to a different set of laws? In either case, what are the laws that govern its behavior? Questions such as these, formulated it is true in widely different ways, are the questions that have pursued psychologists for twenty-five centuries.

The persistent problems of psychology spring from man's attempt to understand his own nature; but when man wonders about himself he must also wonder about that which is not himself. To wonder about the totality of things is to be a philosopher. The persistent problems of psychology, like those of every other science, are thus initially the problems of philosophy. Indeed, it was not until relatively recent times, after the Renaissance, that the several sciences gradually became identified as separate disciplines; and it was not until the late nineteenth century that psychology achieved anything like an independent status. If we are to understand psychology's problems we must consequently see how they have developed in relation to the broader problems of the philosopher.

THE CHALLENGE FROM PHILOSOPHY

In theory, at least, the philosopher is interested in everything, in the nature of the physical world, in the nature of life, in the nature of man, in the standards of correct thinking and of right living, in the meaning of the universe. Traditionally he was the lover of wisdom to whom no field of inquiry was closed, and as recently as the sixteenth century the philosopher could aspire to a mastery of all knowledge. Nowadays, with the tremendous extension of the specialized fields, the philosopher's role has of necessity been constricted; but his basic problems are still the same, and they still include the persistent problems of psychology. In the following analysis we shall identify in drastically simplified fashion the philosophic problems that have had most to do with the initiation of psychological inquiry. In each case the pattern is the same: the philosopher is wrestling with a big problem, like the criteria of truth or the basis of the good life, in trying to solve it he must look at the evidence in human behavior and experience, he becomes interested in the evidence as such, and in the best ways of controlling and verifying his observations; and at this point he has begun to be a psychologist. The psychologist's problem is thus ultimately that of the philosopher, but his immediate concern is with observing and interpreting the facts of behavior and experience. If he is a real psychologist, however, he will never lose sight of the broad problem that lends significance to his observations. The branches of philosophy that have contributed most richly to psychological theory are: metaphysics, epistemology, logic, ethics, aesthetics and politics. Let us take a quick glance at each of these.

(1) *The metaphysical problem.* The term "metaphysics" is an historical accident, referring merely to the writings of Aristotle that came *after* his work on Physics. It is a lucky accident, however, since the word *meta* can also mean *beyond.* The problems of metaphysics are the problems that lie beyond the scope of physical science. What is the nature of ultimate reality? Can we know it? Traditionally, metaphysics has included Ontology (the theory of Being), Epistemology (the theory of Knowledge), Psychology (the theory of the Soul), Theology (the theory of God) and, occasionally, Cosmology (the theory of the Universe). Ontology, Theology and Cosmology need not concern us here. We shall consider the epistemological problem separately, and limit ourselves for the present to the central

metaphysical question that must challenge every psychologist, namely the question as to whether or not man possesses a soul that is distinct from his body.

The philosopher asks: Is there in man a soul (or mind) that is uniquely different from material substance? If so, what is its nature, and how is it related to matter? Are there souls in animals? If there is no soul, how are we to account for the fact that the mental and the material appear to be so different. The most common answers are (a) dualistic or (b) monistic, although there are also (c) pluralistic theories. *Dualism* represents a frank acceptance of two orders of reality as ultimate and irreducible one to the other. The central problem becomes then that of explaining how the two orders are related. Most metaphysicians are impatient with a dualism, however, and struggle for a single principle or a single substance in terms of which everything can be explained. The common monistic theories are: *materialism*, in which mental phenomena are explained as forms or functions of material substance; *idealism*, which accords reality only to the mental; and *neutralism*, which postulates a neutral reality of which mental and material phenomena are merely different manifestations. A *pluralistic* theory would postulate more than two orders of reality, no one of which is to be regarded as more fundamental than any other.

The psychologist as such cannot solve any of these problems, nor can he confirm or refute any metaphysical theory. It is clear, however, that the philosopher in trying to arrive at a meaningful solution must make use of the best possible psychological observation, and that underlying the thinking of the psychologists there must always be at least an implied metaphysical theory.

The psychologist asks: What are the concrete, observable ways in which mental and physical processes are related to one another? What is the precise chain of causation that leads from a physical event (like a stimulus) to a mental response (like a thought or an act), or from a mental event (like a choice) to a consequent change in the physical situation? Questions such as these require detailed studies of the properties of physical stimuli, the behavior of receptors and effectors, the nature of the coordinating mechanisms of the brain, and the relation of all these to the observed facts of experience and behavior; and they require comparative studies of men and animals. The psychologist does not ask, for instance, whether or not animals have souls, but rather in what specific ways the behavior of animals resembles and differs from that of man.

The challenge of metaphysics to psychology is thus to solve the problem of the mind-body relationship. We shall find that this problem has been present in one form or another at every stage in history. In recent years we have tended to subdivide it into: (a) psychophysics, the correlation of mental states with the properties of physical stimuli; (b) psychophysiology, the correlation of mental states with the physiological processes of the organism, particularly of the nervous system; and (c) psychobiology, the study of behavior in the context of the overall characteristics of species, including their evolution. Many modern writers object to the use of terms like "mind" and "mental," contending that these belong properly in metaphysics rather than in science; but, however we state it, the mind-body relationship is present as one of psychology's persistent problems.

(2) *The epistemological and the logical problems.* Epistemology is the philosophic discipline that attempts to determine the nature and validity of knowledge. Logic is the science of correct reasoning. Our theory of knowledge is obviously part and parcel of our general metaphysical theory, and the system of logic we accept is basic to what we do in all branches of philosophy and science. From the point of view of their challenge to psychology, however, they may be grouped together.

The philosopher asks: Can we know the truth, and know with certainty that we know it? By what standards can we distinguish between what is true and what is false? The extreme answers to both questions come from (a) the sceptic, who claims no secure knowledge and doubts even the rules of inference, and (b) the mystic, who believes that truth is directly revealed and requires no logical demonstration. There are few, however, who have tried to defend either extreme position. More commonly, the answers to the epistemological question have tended to fall into two categories, (c) the empiricist, which finds the source of all knowledge in sensory experience, and (d) the rationalist, which postulates a structured mind that imposes its structure on the data of sense. We shall find this alternative pursuing us through the history of psychology.

The answers to the logician's question are less readily classified, but we may note an historical progression from (a) the Aristotelian logic, with its emphasis on deductive method, through (b) the more comprehensive inductive logic required by modern empirical science, with its emphasis on probability statements and the proper methods of generalizing from particular instances, to (c) the currently popular symbolic logic, which is attempting to make logic an extension of mathematics.

Both epistemology and logic are concerned with the problem of knowledge. The philosopher who deals with the problems of knowing must study the processes of knowing; in other words, he must to some extent become a psychologist. Psychology cannot give him his final answer but, if he is to think straight, he must have psychological facts.

The psychologist asks: What are the processes that underlie knowing? What actually happens when we perceive, remember, imagine, understand, think, believe and doubt? These are the psychological problems of cognition, and they have perhaps consumed more energy than have any other problems in the history of psychology. Fifty or seventy-five years ago any systematic treatise on psychology was likely to devote most of its chapters to the analysis of cognition. The historic importance of this field may be explained in part by the intrinsic fascination of its problems; but we can understand it more fully when we realize that for many centuries one's theory of cognition was of crucial practical importance. It required courage to question the authority of revealed religion, and to assert that man has within himself resources that will enable him to obtain true knowledge. To defend a wrong theory of cognition was to place in jeopardy one's career in society, and possibly one's hope for salvation. It is intelligible that the nature of the cognitive processes should have become the object of passionate study.

In recent years the problems of cognition seem to have lost some of their glamour, possibly because society today places less emphasis on orthodoxy of belief than it did a few hundred years ago. There is evidence, however, of a revival of interest in cognition, particularly as its relevance to the psychology of motivation becomes more fully appreciated. If we are to understand why a person does what he does we must know something about the cognitive structure of the world he is living in. Cognition is consequently still a persistent problem.

(3) *The ethical problem.* Ethics, or Moral Philosophy, deals with

the standards in accordance with which conduct can be judged as right or wrong, good or bad. Ethics, like Logic, is a normative discipline, *i.e.*, it attempts to determine what ought to be rather than what is; but it lacks the cleanness and orderliness of Logic. People have little trouble in agreeing upon criteria for sound logical inference; rightness or wrongness in thinking seems to be self-evident. When the question is that of rightness or wrongness of conduct, however, people seldom agree. Moral judgments are evidently too "close to home" to permit of clear thinking. Philosophers have struggled since the beginning of history to make sense of the moral problem; but we are still left with the essential alternatives that were proposed twenty-five centuries ago. Yet the problem persists; for there is no man who is not constantly faced with the question: What ought I to do?

The philosopher asks: What is the nature of the Good Life? What do we mean by "good"? By what standards can we distinguish between "good" and "bad"? Are there "absolutes" in the realm of conduct? The answers are difficult to classify, but they seem to fall into two broad categories: (a) *absolutistic* and (b) *relativistic.* The believer in ethical absolutes may be: (1) an *intuitionist,* who believes that each person possesses an innate conscience or moral sense, possibly implanted by God, which, if unhampered, will judge correctly between right and wrong; or (2) a *rationalist,* who believes that in the natural order of things there is embedded a distinction between what is right and what is wrong—between fitness and unfitness, between appropriateness and inappropriateness, and that clear thinking will of itself lead to a sound moral judgment. The proponent of ethical relativism asserts that no act is in and of itself either right or wrong; its rightness or wrongness can be judged only in the context of its performance. The relativist is impressed by the wide cultural differences in ethical standards. In some cultures all killing, even of animals, is considered wrong; in others, killing in self-defense is condoned but killing for revenge is condemned; and so forth. "Killing" as such is neither right nor wrong; it all depends on the culture.

Whether or not one is an absolutist or a relativist, there is always a fixed criterion by which the rightness or wrongness of conduct is to be judged. It may be "obedience to the will of God," "achievement of happiness," "pleasure," "the greatest good to the greatest number", or, in the case of the extreme relativist, "conformity to custom". In each case a theory of human motivation is required. To defend his theory the moral philosopher must answer the question: Why do people do what they do? Even the intuitionist, who knows the truth, must ask: Why do people not do what they ought to do? Ethical inquiry thus demands psychological fact.

The psychologist asks: What are the processes whereby behavior is actually initiated, directed and regulated? This is the problem of human motivation. The philosopher raises general questions about the nature of conscience, the freedom of the will, egoism versus altruism, the conditions of happiness. The psychologist must reduce these questions to forms that will permit the evidence of observation to speak for itself. What are the observable facts that bear on the experience of self, of self-determination, and of determination by something other than self? What does it feel like to be happy, or needy, or wishful? And how are these feelings related to the ways in which the rest of the world is apprehended? How can conditions be manipulated in such a way as to permit the control of what people do?

The problems of human motivation were set and sustained by man's concern about the problem of ethical judgment. It was not until the late nineteenth century, however, that psychologists began to accept human motivation as a field in which controlled observation could yield substantial fact. Aristotle had laid down his theories; the mediaeval philosophers had interpreted Aristotle in the light of Christian theology; the early modern Protestants had attempted to establish their protest on essentially logical grounds. Charles Darwin presented the field of motivation in a completely new perspective. Darwin's challenge was to look at behavior as it actually occurs in nature. What, he asked, puts organisms into motion? How are external stimuli related to internal states? To what extent is behavior determined by its inborn dispositions? Within what limits can behavior be modified? Instead of speculation, Darwin demanded facts of observation. The result was, as we shall see, that Motivation joined Cognition as a field for empirical inquiry.

There are some who hold that all problems of ethics will ultimately be solved through psychological analysis. Whether or not we accept this position, and this writer does not, we must recognize that any ethical theory demands a psychology of motivation and that the psychologist's interest in motivation is fully meaningful only when it includes the ethical problem.

(4) *The aesthetic problem.* Aesthetics is one of the less clearly articulated of the philosophic disciplines. The Greek root means "to perceive by the senses"; yet in the aesthetic judgment we recognize something more than simple sense-perception. There is something special about a beautiful face, or picture, or scene, or train of argument, that distinguishes it from something ugly. There also seems to be something special about the emotions aroused by beauty that distinguishes them from other emotions. In the Greek tradition Beauty was accepted as one of the three great values in human life, coordinate with Truth and Goodness, and paralleled by the psychological processes of feeling, knowing and willing. Whether these values are distinct or are aspects of a single value, e.g., the Honest Good, whether the aesthetic response is essentially a cognitive or an affective process, become accordingly problems which the philosopher cannot evade. While less attention has been paid to aesthetics than to some of the other philosophic disciplines, every balanced philosophical system contains its aesthetic theory.

The philosopher asks: What are the criteria of the aesthetic judgment? By what standards do we distinguish between the beautiful and the ugly? The common answers may be classified as (a) predominantly *objectivistic* or (b) predominantly *subjectivistic,* although few philosophers would defend a position at either extreme. The two positions represent differing emphases, respectively, on the cognitive content of the aesthetic judgment and on the feeling or emotional content. The objectivist believes he can find the criteria of the aesthetic judgment in the formal properties of things and events. The curve of a line, for instance, the juxtaposition of colors, the patterning or fusion of sounds in melody and harmony, the ordering of ideas in a mathematical demonstration—these are objectively there; and some are aesthetically good, others aesthetically bad. Some objectivists would go as far as to assert that the aesthetic experience is pure precisely when there is no emotional reaction in the observer. The subjectivist claims that the only criterion of the aesthetic is the way we feel when we perceive the object. We may hear a melody or see a pattern of curved lines, but we do not apprehend it as beautiful unless it arouses a special kind of feeling in us. This may be as simple as the diffuse feeling of pleasantness produced by an agreeable odor, or the feeling of repose suggested by a Corot pastoral scene, or it may be as complex as the emotional turmoil aroused by a Tschaikowsky symphony; but the experience is essentially affective. In judging the aesthetic quality of an object we are, according to the subjectivist, merely judging our own feelings. Objectivists are often absolutists, *i.e.,* believing that some things are inherently beautiful and others inherently ugly. Most subjectivists are, at least to some extent, relativists, *i.e.,* holding that what is judged beautiful or ugly is determined primarily by custom, by personal past experience or by accidental circumstance.

Whatever our theoretical preference may be, it is clear that there can be no solution of the aesthetic problem without psychological facts.

The psychologist asks: What happens in a person when he apprehends something as beautiful and something else as ugly? To what extent is his judgment determined by the properties of the object, by his own past experience and by his present motivation? What is the nature of the aesthetic response? What are the conditions of artistic creativity? These are questions that can be answered through the controlled observation of experience and behavior. The psychologist cannot solve the ultimate problem, but he can provide the facts necessary to its clarification.

The problems of aesthetics have always been recognized by psychologists as legitimate, but they seem to have been thrust aside by the apparently more pressing problems of other fields, with the consequence that psychological aesthetics is still in a relatively undeveloped state. One of the reasons is possibly that psychologists share with philosophers a confusion as to precisely what the psychological problems of aesthetics are. Are they essentially cognitive or affective? Or, as a relativistic bias might suggest, should they be approached as special problems of learning? At any rate, here is a field in which philosopher and psychologist must continue to work together for some time to come.

(5) *The political problem.* Here we are using the term "political" in its correct sense, *i.e.,* "having to do with citizenship". Philosophers have traditionally included politics as one of their disciplines. In Ancient Greece the political unit was the city-state; hence the word (Greek *polis* means city). As social organization has become more complex the scope of political philosophy has correspondingly

broadened. What is now called Political Science (perhaps a mis-nomer) deals with the principles of government in all groups that are organized about a set of laws. The problem of politics thus becomes, very broadly stated, the problem of man's place in an ordered society.

The philosopher asks: What is the nature of the State, and what is man's relation to it? What rights and obligations are involved in citizenship? What principles and procedures should be embodied in collective living if man is to achieve the best possible life? These questions clearly have ethical overtones; and, in fact, political philos-ophy has always been close to social ethics. One cannot specify the characteristics of the Good State without having a conception of the Good Life. Political philosophy leads beyond ethics, however, in that it demands facts about social organization. Political science, eco-nomics, history, sociology and cultural anthropology all draw some of their central problems from the philosophy of politics. But there is also a challenge to psychology. Society is an organization of people. If we are to understand the relation between the individual and his society we must know the facts of social behavior. Every political philosophy has contained, explicitly or implicitly, a social psychology.

Political theories are even less easy to classify than are the theories of moral and aesthetic judgment. Plato gives us a fivefold classifica-tion of the types of state: aristocracy (rule by the wisest), timocracy (rule by those who are "looked up to"), oligarchy (rule by "the few," obviously those who have attained wealth and power), democ-racy (rule by the many, most of whom are poor and irresponsible), and tyranny (rule by a single dictator). Plato favored the aristocracy. Subsequent history has witnessed many a conflict in the realm of political theory, *e.g.*, absolute versus limited monarchy, the monarch-ical versus the republican system, decision by experts versus decision by majority vote, each of which might be restated in the language of Plato's analysis. Contemporary thinking seems to tend toward one or other of two extremes: (a) dictatorship emphasis on centralized authority, with a high degree of social regulation directed by a small group of individuals; and (b) anarchy emphasis on maximum inde-pendence for the individual, with a minimum of regulation by law. Neither extreme is, of course, ever actually achieved, nor is either often advocated. All political theorists recognize that some degree of social regulation is necessary, and most pay at least lip-service to the value of individual liberty. What is of psychological interest is the fact that each position involves certain identifiable assumptions about the nature of human nature. The advocate of individualism, for instance, must assume that man is in some measure capable of free and rational choice; otherwise his state would be a chaos. The socialist must assume that human nature can be changed. Both must make assumptions about individual differences, about human motives, about the learning process. In other words, although the psychologist cannot solve the ultimate problem of political philosophy, he can provide some of the facts that are essential to political theorizing.

The psychologist asks: What makes man behave as a social being? Is he innately gregarious? innately acquisitive? Are all men born with the same capabilities and tendencies? To what extent is man moulded into what he is by the forces of society? What makes one man a leader and another a follower? Are there laws of group behavior that differ from those of individual behavior?

Since the days of Plato virtually all possible theoretical answers to these questions have been offered. It is only recently, however, that psychologists have begun to derive their answers from a systematic scrutiny of the facts of social behavior. Social psychology is consequently one of the less disciplined of the psychological specialities. Nevertheless, as we shall see, considerable progress has been made. The psychology of individual differences is developing more and more rigorous statistical methods; the psychology of motivation is becoming oriented towards the problems of behavior in social contexts; the students of learning are beginning to wrestle with the problems of socialization; human communication is being accepted as a field for factual research; and the toughest problem of all, that of the development and organization of the personality, is slowly becoming clarified. We cannot say that the problem of man in society is a single psychological problem. It is a cluster of problems, all of which have persisted through the centuries, and all of which are vigorously alive today.

2

The Classic Doctrines
of
Man

WHAT WE MEAN BY A DOCTRINE OF MAN

WE HAVE SEEN that the persistent problems of psychology arise initially as problems of philosophy. The thinker, attempting to grapple with the ultimate problems of reality, of knowledge and of human values, finds himself asking concrete questions about human experience and human behavior. He finds himself observing, classifying in different ways, trying to discover what causes what. He may have little faith that observation alone will furnish him with final answers, but he realizes that acquaintance with fact will at least clarify his thinking and enable him to make more intelligent guesses. Sometimes he finds himself becoming interested in the facts as such, and trying to order within his system not merely some of the facts, but all the facts of behavior and experience. At this point he is beginning to be a psychologist. Within the context of his philosophic system, he is beginning to think of man as such as a problem of investigation, worthy of study, even if that study leads only to partial understanding.

It is clear that the attempt to develop a consistent and intelligible picture of man will always be influenced by the systematic assumptions of the thinker. Different thinkers may agree on the facts—although they seldom do completely—but their interpretation of those facts will inevitably be colored by their convictions as to what is ultimately true and important. The trained philosopher will make these assumptions explicit, indicating why he accepts this fact as

43

important and rejects that one. In the thinking of the philosophically naive man these assumptions are likely to be unrecognized; but they are none the less there, and they will dictate the final interpretation he will give to the facts. It is natural, then, that as thinkers have sought a consistent interpretation of man their conclusions should have tended to conform to a number of different patterns, corresponding to the different explicit or implicit assumptions brought to the inquiry by the thinker.

We may consequently expect that, as we pursue the developing quest for an understanding of man, we shall find a number of alternative ways in which man can be understood, each perhaps consistent within itself, but each differing in some significant way from the others. We shall refer to these self-consistent interpretations as *doctrines of man.* Since they are dictated in part by assumptions which we cannot challenge, we shall not be in a position to demonstrate that one is right and another wrong. The best we can do is to try to identify these assumptions, to be clear as to the ways in which facts are related to assumptions, and to make our final choice ourselves in the light of what we consider to be important. As scientists we shall have to suspend our final judgment but, also as scientists, we cannot honestly overlook the fact that thoughtful people have honestly come to different conclusions.

The alternative doctrines of man may be classified and subclassified in many ways. For the sake of simplicity we shall identify them as they emerged in the early history of psychology. We shall call these the *classic doctrines of man.* It is perhaps no accident that as the Greeks and early Christians wrestled with the problem of understanding man's place in the universe they should have propounded at varying times five significantly different ways in which man can be understood. Each of these has survived the test of history. Each has absorbed the content furnished by fresh thought and new discovery, but each still stands as a challenge to curiosity.

In the attempt to understand any specific theory or general doctrine it is helpful to keep four criteria in mind. These are:

(1) *Problem.* What are the problems that the writer is trying to solve? What is it that he is really curious about? We shall find that many apparently irreconcilable psychological theories are really theories about different problems. Their proponents are curious about different things. One may be concerned about the basis of the

aesthetic judgment, another about the prediction and control of behavior, still another about the resolution of emotional conflicts. Each may condemn the others as wrong; whereas the truth may be simply that their fields of interest are not the same.

(2) *Data.* A *datum* is that which is given. Every scientist must have data which he accepts as legitimate and from which he works. Data are the things he looks at and tries to explain. But the data of the astronomer are not the data of the chemist or the biologist. Each science selects from all the "givens" of observation those that are relevant to its peculiar problems. For the astronomer the records of the successive positions of stars are data; but not the reproductive cycles of birds. For the biologist the records of bird migrations are data, but not the interactions of different chemical substances. The data of psychology have never been fully agreed upon. For some psychologists the primary data are the elementary facts of consciousness; for others they are the objectively observable facts of behavior. The selection may depend on the problem the psychologist is interested in. We cannot decide at this point that one kind of datum is right and the other wrong; but we must recognize that our theoretical bias may determine in advance of our observation what data we are prepared to accept.

(3) *Methods.* Every science has its methods of observing, of generalizing, of verifying and of drawing inferences. Some of these, like the methods of logical inference, are almost universal, challenged only by the mystics. Others, like the method of controlled experimentation, are appropriate to some sciences, but not to others; the astronomer, for instance, cannot perform controlled experiments with the stars. Still other methods, and these are sometimes called techniques, are appropriate only to the special data of a particular science. The microscope, for instance, is indispensable to the histologist but not to the sociologist; the intensive interview is essential to cultural anthropology, but not to physical chemistry. The methods are thus in part dictated by the problems and the data of the science.

Methods may, however, limit, direct or liberate the activity of the scientist; and this has been particularly true of psychology. The Scholastic method (cf. p. 82) involved a disparagement of empirical inquiry. The experimental method of the post-Renaissance period (cf. pp. 171f.f.) opened out new vistas, as did the statistical methods of the twentieth century; but at the same time they disparaged the evidence of intuition. New methods usually reveal new phenomena that stimulate curiosity. Sometimes established methods act as blinders, restricting the view of the scientist. We shall see in our review of the story of psychology that the general acceptance of a method has frequently impeded the progress of the science.

(4) *Constructs.* When the scientist is solving his problem he is reducing the problematical to the obvious; in other words, he is explaining it. To explain is, literally, to make clear. When we make something clear we relate it to other facts of experience, which we have accepted, in such a way that it no longer puzzles us. Constructs are postulated entities or processes which we do not know directly but which we have come to believe in, and which consequently possess explanatory value. No one has seen an electron or a gene with the naked eye, yet we believe in their existence, and we use them in our explanation of physical and biological phenomena.

Electrons, protons, genes, vitamins and the polio virus are all constructs which most of us accept as real existents in terms of which natural phenomena can be explained. In psychology we have similar constructs such as: the faculty of reason, the will, the senses, associative bonds, the instincts, primary drives, stimulus-response connections, the superego, cortical traces, habit-family-hierarchies, autochthonous organization, and so forth. None of these is a directly observable thing or process, but each has been accepted by some psychologists as representing something real and as having explanatory value. Some of our confusion in the understanding of different psychological systems is due to the fact that different explanatory constructs are accepted. In the physical sciences the explanatory constructs have been fairly well agreed upon. In psychology there is still turmoil. Some psychologists insist on a neurophysiological explanation of psychological phenomena; others prefer to look for the understanding of behavior in early childhood experience; still others feel that man can be understood only in the context of the social forces that play upon him; and so forth. In any case, it is clear that we cannot comprehend any psychological system until we know which particular constructs it accepts as explanatory.

Thus we can see that the problems of psychology may determine its data, that its data may determine its methods, and that all three may determine its constructs; but also that each of the four may affect all of the others. If we are to understand a psychological system we must know what the psychologist is curious about, what data he is willing to accept as relevant, what methods are for him legitimate, and what satisfied him as an explanation.

THE BACKGROUND OF ANCIENT GREECE

Among the culturally creative periods of history, perhaps the most impressive is the stretch from approximately 600 B.C. to approximately 300 B.C. in Greece. The scientific student of history will continue to wonder about the conditions of cultural creativity. Is it to be understood in terms of climate, social organization, ease of communication, fertilizing contacts with other cultures? Is there a natural life cycle for cultures, analogous to those of organisms? Whatever the explanation, a scant three hundred years of Greek history provide us with an unparalleled example of cultural creativity. During this period, particularly in Athens, there were stirring developments in mathematics and the physical sciences; the arts of the poet, the dramatist and the musician flourished; the theory of the democratic state was tested in practice; and all the great philosophic systems had their birth. During this period we have the first recorded attempts to explain the nature of man and his place in the universe. Our first systematic psychology thus stems from the Greeks.

Human curiosity, when awakened, spontaneously turns outward. The early Greeks seem to have been puzzled first by the phenomena of physical nature. How is it constituted? How explain its transformations, like growth, decay and whatever happens when things burn? Are there fixed elements, like earth, air, fire and water; or are there innumerable elements? Thales, Anaximander, Anaximenes, Anaxagoras, Empedocles—all propounded physical theories of the world. But they could not be content with a mere reduction to elements. They recognized that elements, when combined, must be combined in accordance with a principle, or even a plan. To account for the order of nature one must assume an ordering principle, perhaps even an ordering mind. *Logos*—the principle of reason, *Nous*—the guiding mind; these were invoked to explain the order of nature. For some thinkers the fact of change was most important (Heraclitus: You can never step twice into the same stream); for others, *e.g.*, Parmenides, it was the permanence behind change that was impressive. Even change in nature is change in accordance with rule. If we are to understand reality we must understand the "rules"; we must seek behind appearances for that which is real and enduring.

The early Greeks were seeking for a simple way in which nature and life could be understood. Some writers have referred to this early period as the hylozoistic period, a period during which they sought a *"bule,"* or fundamental substance, which could be united with a *"zoe,"* or principle of life. The hylozoists were pioneer scientists. They looked outward upon the world and tried to find a reasonable explanation for it. Yet they realized, perhaps dimly, that they the theorists had something to do with the nature of the theories they were building. The early Greeks gave us theories of nature, but implicit in their theories was the thought that man, the theorist, might be an integral part of the process of theory building. Greek curiosity naturally and inevitably became focussed upon man.

The historians sometimes call this second period the anthropological period, the period during which scientific inquiry gradually became directed toward the study of man, and philosophers began to appreciate the role of the human factor in the direction of philosophic thought. This is probably an oversimplification, since Greek philosophers at all times included man in their attempts to explain nature. Nevertheless, about the beginning of the 5th century B.C., there emerged a group of teachers, known as the Sophists (wise men), who courageously challenged the traditions of their elders, and kept insisting that philosophic, i.e., scientific, inquiry should begin with the study of man. How can one develop a theory of the world, they asked, without first scrutinizing the processes whereby one perceives and thinks? The Sophists were rebels; they were iconoclasts. They are frequently charged with having been more concerned with the splitting of hairs than with the attainment of truth—witness our current epithet "sophistry" for the argument that obscures the essentials with logically sound trivialities. Nevertheless, it was the Sophists who for the first time made human experience and behavior a legitimate subject for scientific inquiry.

PROTAGORAS, AND THE RELATIVISTIC DOCTRINE OF MAN

The greatest of the Sophists was undoubtedly Protagoras (480–411 B.C.). Born in the Thracian town of Abdera, he spent the bulk of his adult life in Athens, and there crossed swords with the best of the Athenian philosophers. He was eventually expelled as a heretic and died an expatriate. Others of the Sophists have come down in history, e.g., Gorgias, but Protagoras is the best representative of the relativistic doctrine of man.

"Man is the measure of all things." This is the quotation for which Protagoras is famous. To paraphrase, "Everything that we know is in part a function of the knowing agent." The data of direct experience may be accepted as such; what is not given in direct experience must always be questioned. Protagoras kept insisting, on the one hand, that the scientist should never depart from the available data, on the other hand that he should scrutinize the available data and squeeze them for what they are worth. The implication is that knowledge may extend beyond immediate experience, but that, in the last analysis, the intents and the limitations of the thinker will determine the nature of the product.

The Protagorean doctrine dramatizes a distinction that runs through Greek philosophy—indeed, through all philosophy—namely, the distinction between appearance and reality. Appearances (*phenomena*, in the correct sense of the term) are the familiar things, events and relationships of everyday perception. That appearances are deceptive is a truism. The stick in the water appears bent; the tiny cavity in the tooth feels large to the tongue; the mirage in the desert, the hallucinations of the insane, the faces in the clouds—all are appearances that are clearly at variance with reality. If our direct experience is limited to appearances, how can we discover what is real? Sometimes we think we have adequate tests. We can withdraw the stick from the water and see that it is "really" straight; we can look at the tooth cavity in a mirror and see that it is "really" small. When we do so, however, we are merely substituting one percept for another; the second percept, however more satisfying it may be, is no less an appearance than is the first. Even when we demonstrate a high degree of coherence among our percepts, we have no assurance that we are perceiving what is really there. At best, said Protagoras, we can have an opinion; even if we have true knowledge we can never know that it is true.

The challenge of Protagoras is even more disturbing when we leave the realm of simple perception and begin to construct theories. Just as what I perceive is a function of my powers of perception, so what I think is a function of my thought processes. The wish, says the proverb, is father to the thought. It is easier for me to hate my enemy if I think he is utterly bad; I feel more comfortable if I can resign my major decisions to an all-wise God. Therefore I believe in God, and accept as fact everything bad that is said about my enemy. To carry the thought even further: if I had no eyes, there would be no world of color; if I lacked the capacity to appreciate the relation between cause and effect, the sequence of events would have a different meaning. The world of the worm is limited to what the worm can perceive and comprehend; the world of man is structured by the capacities and motives of man. The perceiver and thinker can never transcend his own perceiving and thinking processes.

Protagoras presents us with a relativistic philosophy, with man as the inescapable determiner of all relations. Philosophers have responded to relativism with two types of answer. One answer, scepticism, is defeatist. The sceptic simply concedes that he does not know anything; his brother, the agnostic, asserts not merely that he does not know anything but that he cannot know anything. Both can be easily tripped. We can ask the question: Is the statement, "I do not know anything," a true statement? The agnostic must answer "yes," in which case he has affirmed a truth and denied his position. If the sceptic answers with "I do not know whether or not I know anything," he is then asked the further question, "Is it true that you do not know?" And so *ad infinitum.* But there have been no really sceptical philosophers. The more common response of philosophers has been to try to find within the data of experience a justification for the transcending of experience. The very phenomena (appearances) themselves, they say, require us to believe in the existence of a reality that is nonphenomenal and about which we can make true statements. And these statements, they add, are not dictated by man's perceiving and thinking processes; they represent, rather, the accommodation of man's perception and thought to what is independent of man's perceiving and thinking. What is independent may be conceived as of the nature of mind, as of the nature of matter, or as a neutral reality that is neither mind nor matter. We shall see how these different alternatives have affected psychological theory.

The direct consequences of relativism for psychological theory may be recognized in three types of emphasis that have recurred from time to time in the history of our subject. We shall term these (1) phenomenalism, (2) projection theory, and (3) introjection theory. Each is a logically definable position which in actual fact is seldom defended without reservation or compromise.

The *phenomenalist* would accept at face value the Protagoran thesis that the individual cannot transcend the world of appearances, but would argue that appearances (phenomena) are worth studying in their own right. For him, psychology can be nothing more than the observation, description and classification of phenomena. Since we can have no independent knowledge of an external world, of a deity or of any other postulated reality, it is fruitless to try to correlate phenomena with the constructs of the other sciences. In fact, the consistent phenomenalist would have to argue that, since the pointer-readings of the physicist or astronomer, the observations of the biologist and the conceptualizations of the historian are all in the last analysis human experiences, therefore these sciences can represent nothing more than the ordering of arbitrary selections of phenomena. From this point of view, each of the other sciences must be regarded as a subdivision of psychology. While such a thesis has been occasionally advanced, it has never won many followers.

The *projection theorist* takes as his starting point the motivated individual, and proceeds to demonstrate the relativity of all other psychological phenomena to the inescapable fact of motivation. We believe what we wish to believe, we accept as legitimate goals of conduct only those that are consonant with our basic needs, we perceive even the size and color of objects in accordance with their "value" to us. The world as man apprehends it is merely an outward projection of man's inner needs, desires, aspirations and anxieties. God, the projectionist would assert, was made in the image of man, not man in the image of God.

One of the best examples of projection is the ink blot test, developed and standardized by the Swiss psychiatrist, Rorschach. A sheet of paper on which some ink has been dropped is folded over. As the ink runs and spreads in all directions it assumes fantastic configurations. The subject, looking at it, may see people, animals, flowers, things which threaten or reassure, scenes of activity or repose—the possibilities are almost limitless. Rorschach found that what you see seems to depend on the kind of person you are. It is as though you project into the ink blot the essential characteristics of yourself. In a similar way a picture—the Thematic Apperception Test—will yield from different people widely different stories, each person "projecting" into the picture a meaning that reveals his own inner propensities and conflicts. In the same way, we "see" faces as threatening if we feel threatened or as friendly if we feel secure (the Szondi test); we fill the blanks in an incomplete sentence with words that betray our dominant concerns (the Sentence Completion Test); and, in memory, we exaggerate or diminish in size the image of a person with whom we have had dealings, the size depending on the nature of our relation with him. There seems to be ample evidence to support the judgment that the way things appear to us depends in important ways on the way in which we ourselves are organized.

Projection theory is thus a relativism of the world to the individual. Its basic datum is the motivated individual, and it sees the world as a projection—a throwing out—of the individual's characteristics. Psychology, from this point of view, is an expansion of the theory of motivation.

Introjection theory is the opposite of projection theory. It is a relativism of the individual to the world. Its most common expression is in the theory of cultural relativity, a doctrine which has recently received considerable support from anthropological researches. The introjection theorist sees the individual as a creature of his culture. It is a fact of common observation that people of approximately the same biological constitution, but born and reared in different cultures, develop in accordance with the pattern of their culture. They learn the same language, dress in the same way, conform to the same patterns of eating, housing and mating, and accept the same standards of truth, goodness and beauty. In spite of occasional individual variation, the "pattern" or "theme" of the culture seems to be the dominant shaping influence. It would appear that the really fundamental things about a person are dictated by the culture in which he develops, that the individual is merely a partial expression of something that is much bigger than himself.

One of the best examples of introjection theory is to be found in the study of language. Language is a distinctly human achievement.

In spite of all the efforts of animal psychologists, no subhuman animal has ever mastered the technique of symbolizing by sounds or gestures the complex things, events and relationships of the world in which we live. Yet language is a learned activity. The language that the individual learns is there before the individual is born. No individual ever masters it completely. What the individual does is accommodate himself partially to a linguistic system that is already lodged in his culture. He learns to recognize objects for which there are names, to recognize attributes for which there are adjectives, to think in terms of concepts for which the language has provided symbols. It is a fascinating question whether the individual can ever in his thinking transcend the concepts laid down for him by his language. It might look as though what is most distinctively human about man is absorbed from his culture.

The introjection theory is thus a learning-oriented theory. Man is to be conceived, not as a dynamo of energy, dictating and shaping his world, but as a lump of putty, conforming to pressures that come from without. The individual becomes an individual as he is battered into shape by forces over which he has no control.

DEMOCRITUS, AND THE MATERIALISTIC DOCTRINE OF MAN

Perhaps the easiest, and certainly the most popular, escape from relativism is by way of materialism. The materialist argues that basic reality is of the nature of matter, and that the phenomena regarded as mental are merely other forms of material substance. The materialist philosophy had its followers among the Greeks, and in one form or another it has been accepted as a working philosophy by possibly a majority of modern scientists.

Our Greek example of the systematic materialist is Democritus (ca. 460– ca. B.C. 370). Little is known of his life other than that he, like Protagoras, was born in Abdera, that he traveled widely, but that unlike Protagoras he preferred a life of quiet contemplation to the rough and tumble disputations of busy Athens. Only fragments of his writings have come down to us, but these are impressive. The evidence indicates that many centuries before the emergence of modern atomic physics Democritus had conceived of the universe as composed of an infinite number of small, indivisible, indestructible units ("atom" means "uncuttable"), differing only in size, shape, weight and motion. The popular belief before Democritus was in four fundamental but essentially different types of substance—earth, air, fire and water—the mixture of which in varying proportions could account for all the phenomena of nature. But Democritus with his passion for simplicity could not rest content with a pluralism of elements. There must, he believed, be one primary substance to which everything can be reduced. This substance might take different forms and behave in different ways, but there must be an underlying unity to nature. The explanation of nature must ultimately be in terms of what we now call physics. In the last analysis there can be no laws other than the laws of physical science.

This is the essence of the materialist position. But how does the materialist account for the phenomena of mind? For Democritus the answer lay in the atoms. Atoms are indivisible and indestructible, but they differ in size, shape and motion. Some atoms are smaller, smoother and livelier than others. These are the "soul" atoms. When a person thinks, the "soul" atoms are agitated; when he wills the motion is transmitted outward; when he perceives, atoms from the outside world pass through the sense organs and set up similar motions in the "soul" atoms. Thus the apparent difference between the mental and the physical is overcome. Mind and matter are essentially the same, mind being merely a subtler form of matter.

Democritus was first and foremost a physicist, but he seems to have developed a fairly complete psychology within the limits of his atomic theory, even assigning different psychological functions to different parts of the body—thought to the brain, anger to the heart, appetite to the liver—and he found the secret of the good life in gentle motions of the soul-atoms. Our interest, however, is less in his specific conclusions than in the broad doctrine of man he presents. For Democritus, man is a part of physical nature, to be explained in terms of physical laws. His psychology is the prototype of a psychology that has been popular for more than two hundred years.

Modern materialism cannot be pigeon holed, for it has taken many forms; but, as we shall see later, the materialistic doctrine of man has assumed a fairly standard pattern. Here are a few of its common characteristics:

(1) *Materialism is monistic.* It rejects any ultimate distinction between mind and matter, and asserts that matter is the fundamental reality, and that everything can ultimately be explained in terms of physical law.

(2) *Materialism is Usually Atomistic.* It attempts to reduce the complex to the simple, the large to the small. With each subdivision of matter into smaller parts, it has accepted the small parts as more fundamental than their larger configurations. Thus the molecule is less fundamental than are its constituent atoms and, now that the atom has been broken down into electrons, protons, anti-protons, neutrons, etc., these are regarded as more fundamental than the atoms.

(3) *Materialism Reduces Quality to Quantity.* The world of experience gives us qualities like red and blue, sweet and sour, warm and cold. Materialism seeks to translate these into differences in wavelength of light, chemical reaction to receptors, transmission of molecular motion. The qualities are regarded as secondary, to be restated eventually as quantitative differences in the behavior of a single primary substance.

(4) *Materialism Reduces Function to Structure.* Organisms behave as though they were trying to maintain themselves, seeking appropriate food, defending themselves against danger, selecting mates and reproducing their kind. These are organismic functions which look as though they revealed an organismic purpose. From the materialist point of view, purpose cannot exist in nature. Such apparently purposive functions must be explained in terms of structures which have evolved, possibly as a result of natural selection, in such a way that the species is preserved. It is the structure that is inherited or that is built up through learning. The structure of the eye, for example, which permits us to discriminate colors, forms and movements, must be the end product of an evolutionary process; and similarly the fine distinctions of the logician must in the last analysis be referred to structural relations among the cortical elements.

(5) *Materialism Attempts to Explain the Psychological in Terms of the Non-Psychological.* Although it may admit such traditional psychological terms as perceiving, remembering, thinking and choosing as occasionally useful for descriptive purposes, it insists that a proper explanation must use constructs drawn from a more basic

science. Usually, although not always, this science is neurophysiology. Thus, memory might be explained as the persistence of changes in synaptic resistance, choice as the result of the dominance of one efferent pathway over another. So far as psychology is concerned the reduction to terms of neurophysiology is usually considered sufficient. For the consistent materialist, however, this reduction is only a first step towards a complete scientific explanation. Further reductions would in succession involve restatements in the language of even more fundamental sciences, *e.g.,* biochemistry, physical chemistry, until finally the level of physics had been achieved. Every materialist will concede that no such complete reduction is yet possible. Nevertheless, such is his faith in the unity of science that he is willing to accept it as a legitimate goal.

The materialistic doctrine of man in Ancient Greece did not long survive Democritus. As we shall see, an alternative doctrine propounded by Plato found readier followers, and the grand synthesis of Aristotle, reinterpreted by the Christian Church, was to dominate the thinking of the western world for many centuries. The materialist faith in physical science was never completely lost, but in an intellectual world ruled by the theologians a frank materialism came to be regarded as a heresy of the worst sort. With the emergence of the new science of the sixteenth century a materialistic account of physical nature began to appear possible, but it was not until the eighteenth and nineteenth centuries that any serious efforts were made to reestablish it as a doctrine of man.

Modern materialism in psychology began with the Newtonian revolution in physics, gained strength as Darwin began to close the gap between man and animal, and must now be regarded as the doctrine of man most generally accepted by scientists. True, the conception of matter is being drastically revised by modern physicists, but the prevailing materialist view is that, however we conceive of matter, there is nothing in the structure or functioning of man that cannot eventually be restated in terms of physical law. Whether we use the language of stimuli and responses, the language of cell-assemblies and reverberating circuits or some new language still to be invented, it is part of the faith of the materialist that physical science can ultimately be extended to include all the phenomena of human behavior and experience.

PLATO, AND THE IDEALISTIC DOCTRINE OF MAN

Simple, massive and convincing as was the materialism of Democritus, it was a radically different alternative to the relativistic doctrine of man that appealed most strongly to the Greeks. Not the physical but the mental, not matter but reason, promised to furnish the laws in terms of which man and his relation to the universe could be understood. The system became known as Idealism, a system that encompassed not merely psychology but also all the other basic philosophic disciplines and that was destined to guide a great tradition that has continued to the present. Idealism as a system of thought is not to be confused with the tender-minded, occasionally overemotional, belief in ideals commonly attributed to impetuous youth. Greek idealism asserted that the Idea, the rationally derived concept, is the fundamental element of reality, that the material world is only a partial expression, even a degradation, of the world of ideas. Man, from the point of view of the idealist, is a partial embodiment of ideal realities that transcend the world of matter.

The great spokesman for Greek Idealism is Plato (427–347 B.C.), but the thinking of Plato can never be divorced from that of his teacher, Socrates (ca. 470–399 B.C.). Socrates might be listed as one of the Sophists, *i.e.,* as a member of the new profession of teachers who contributed so richly to the intellectual life of Athens during the fifth century BC. Like many other Sophists he preferred the informal discussion to the formal lecture, the corner in the market-place or the friendly shade of a tree to the formal classroom. He thought of himself as a "spiritual midwife," whose privilege it was to assist his pupils in the birth of their ideas. Sometimes the birth was painful, and sometimes the product was a monstrosity, but Socrates had faith in the process of reasoning. Through the dialogues of Plato we gain the impression of Socrates as a gentle, humble, but diabolically ingenious debater. From the Dialogues, but especially from the *Apology,* we also gain the impression of a man whose devotion to truth conquered even the fear of death. After a lifetime of service to Athens, Socrates was condemned to death by his fellow-citizens as a subversive influence. He defended himself nobly (*The Apology*), but when the emotional jury rejected his defense he accepted the verdict and drank the prescribed poison.

It is difficult to untangle the thinking of Socrates from that of Plato, for most of what we know of Socrates comes from Plato. It is clear, however, that Socrates challenged both the relativistic and the materialistic doctrine of man. He believed that reason was not only a capacity of man, but a force that could penetrate through appearances and reveal reality in its true form. There is no moral problem, he insisted, that cannot be solved by clear thinking. In the last analysis, virtue and knowledge are one. Like Protagoras, he believed that the first duty of the scientist is to understand himself; but, unlike Protagoras, he believed that self-knowledge contains within itself the means whereby the world of appearances can be transcended. One of the most interesting of Plato's Dialogues is the *Protagoras,* in which Socrates is presented as the opponent of relativism. How much is Socrates and how much is Plato, we cannot say; but, at least, we have here Plato's answer to the relativistic challenge.

Plato was a pupil of Socrates. In many a street-corner debate he must have sharpened his wits in a Socratic dialogue. It is certain that he drew much of his inspiration, and perhaps his basic philosophy, from Socrates; but it is equally clear that he went far beyond Socrates in his attempt to build a complete system of philosophy. Plato eventually founded his own school, "The Academy," taught his own students (of whom the most distinguished was Aristotle), and published the results of his thinking in what have come to be recognized as among the world's greatest contributions to literature and philosophy. The form of the dialogue had been laid down by the great Greek dramatists, Aeschylus, Sophocles and Euripides, and it is intelligible that Plato should have accepted the dialogue as his medium and have selected Socrates as his chief protagonist. It is equally interesting, however, that as Plato grew older, although Socrates was usually the chief spokesman, the dialogues gradually turned into monologues. Plato the systematist was supplanting Plato the artist. In the writings of both the artist and the systematist, however, we find the essence of the idealistic doctrine of man.

For the idealist the inescapable fact about man is that he can think, and that by clear thinking he can discern the reality behind appearances. Thinking, then, not mere observation, is the true instrument of science; and the finest example of science is obviously mathematics. In mathematics we may have to compromise with appearances when we use algebraic symbols and geometric designs, but the sensory content of these is irrelevant. It matters little whether we use x or y, alpha or beta, to represent a quantity, whether we convey the notion of triangularity by red or green, thick or thin lines. The idea of quantity or of triangularity is what is essential, and the more skilled we become the less we depend on sensory supports. Any triangle we may draw is imperfect, but this does not hinder us from grasping the essence of triangularity. In mathematics we come closest to commerce with pure ideas.

Science from the idealist's point of view is thus a discovery. The ideas are there to begin with as the essential structure of reality. The philosopher (scientist) is the one who can apprehend the ideas most clearly. The ideas of causality, of opposition, of beauty and of goodness, are not products of the scientist's thinking; they are part of the reality that is gradually becoming known to him. His knowledge can never be complete, for reality contains more ideas than the human mind can ever grasp, but he has in the inner consistency of his own thinking an indication as to whether or not he is on the right track. Truth is there for us, and it is up to us to learn how to recognize it.

Plato's doctrine of man is built on the assumption that man is a rational being who through reason can come to a knowledge of reality, but whose reason is often disorganized by irrational forces. From Plato we have inherited the famous doctrine of "the faculties," a doctrine that has had a long and honorable history, that is now generally rejected, but that has had such a universal appeal that it cannot be lightly discarded. The novelist may still say, "His emotions got the better of his reason," the political reporter may still contrast a "rational" with an "emotional" appeal, and from the pulpit we are still enjoined to keep our "lower impulses" under control. The Platonic doctrine was altered somewhat by the Christians, but it is still with us. When in our judgements of ourselves and others we distinguish between "rational" and "irrational," between "higher" and "lower," we are speaking the language of Plato.

Plato's doctrine of man comes out most clearly in the *Republic*. No idealist can divorce his psychology from his ethics, aesthetics, epistemology and metaphysics. In the *Republic* it is the problem of social ethics that absorbs Plato, and in trying to solve it he presents his psychology. What, he asks, is the nature of justice?

Justice is a social concept, that demands a theory of society. Through the wit and wisdom of Socrates, Plato examines and deflates all the standard theories of social justice, justice as the interest of the stronger, justice as a social compromise, and so forth. He concludes that the principles that underlie the just state must reflect the principles in accordance with which the individual attains the Good Life. What are these principles? In the good state there are three classes of people: the workers, who cannot be entrusted with many decisions, and whose virtues are industry and sobriety; the soldiers (auxiliaries), who must defend the state and whose virtue is courage; and the philosopher-kings (guardians) who make the decisions, and whose virtue is wisdom. Thus in the ideal state there are those who think, those who enforce the decisions of the thinkers, and those who do the work. It is a good state when all elements are in harmony with one another, with the wise men taking the lead.[1]

The state is, however, really a reflection of the nature of the individual. Corresponding to the three classes of society there are in the human soul three fundamental divisions of powers, appetite, spirit and reason. If the Good Life is to be achieved, reason, supported by spirit, must maintain control over appetite. In Plato we have the finest statement of the Greek ideal of the Life of Reason as the highest goal of man.

Let us take a closer look at each of the three parts of the soul as Plato describes them.

(1) The appetitive part is man's lower nature, and Plato characteristically locates the appetites in the lower portions of the body. In modern terminology the appetites might be labelled as instincts, primary drives or basic needs. In the Freudian system they are assigned to the Id. The appetites cannot be disregarded, for they are essential to living; but they are irrational, and they must be kept under control. Unbridled hunger leads to gluttony, and unbridled lust to lechery. Just as a state that is dominated by the mob will

---

[1] One cannot resist the famous quotation from Jowett's translation of the *Republic* (Book V, 473): "Until philosophers are kings, or the kings and princes of this world have the spirit and power of philosophy, and political greatness and wisdom meet in one, and those commoner natures who pursue either to the exclusion of the other are compelled to stand aside, cities will never have rest from their evils,—no, nor the human race, as I believe—and then only will this our state have a possibility of life and behold the light of day."

subside into chaos, so the individual who allows his appetites to rule him will disintegrate.

(2) The spirited part is a little more difficult to identify, but Plato seems to have had in mind the power in man that gives him courage. He located it in the heart, and in his social analogue he likened it to the soldier class. Soldiers are characteristically brave, energetic and adventurous; they impose discipline on the masses while protecting them, but they also accept orders in disciplined fashion from their superiors. In Plato's thinking man's spirit was linked with his reason as part of his higher nature. It accounts for ambition, tenacity of purpose, defiance of danger. Like a spirited stallion, it can carry one to victory; but, also like the stallion, it can run wild and create havoc, unless it has a skillful rider.

(3) The rational faculty is man's supreme endowment. Through reason man can attain truth, recognize beauty and achieve the Good Life. Reason enables man to penetrate the world of appearances and grasp the real world of Ideas. Like Democritus, Plato located reason in the head (possibly, it is suggested, because the head is the most nearly spherical portion of the body, and the sphere is the mathematically perfect figure), but its location in the body is unimportant. Reason is the highest faculty of an immaterial and immortal soul. When the soul takes up residence in the body it is inevitably hampered, and sometimes degraded, by the association; but it can through reason progress towards emancipation. When man achieves the Life of Reason he has conquered his appetites and is living in the World of Ideas.

The details of Plato's philosophy need not concern us here. It is an interpretation of reality as ideal rather than as material. There is also much in Plato's psychology that does not merit close examination. In the *Theaetetus,* for instance, he gives us a theory of perception that bears little relation to the facts as we know them, in the *Cratylus* a theory of language that no competent linguist would entertain, in the *Timaeus,* a highly mythical account of the origin of bodily structures and functions. He was most ingenious in his speculations but, as compared, for instance, with Aristotle, he was lamentably weak in his observation. For the idealist, however, the test of truth is not the brute fact of observation but the subtle distinction that survives the scrutiny of reason. The idealist is not prejudiced against the observation of natural phenomena, but he insists that nature can reveal truth only when it is thought about. Plato, the idealist, believed that the final truth about man must come from clear thinking.

There are few contemporary psychologists who could identify themselves as idealists, and still fewer who would call themselves Platonists. Idealism is not popular today. Nevertheless there is much in modern psychology which, possibly unrecognized, is reminiscent of Plato's doctrine of man. Plato's conception of the human soul as an immaterial entity that pre-exists, takes temporary residence in a body, and then when the body dies flits to another body in another world, has been incorporated into many theological systems, but in recent times it has seldom found favor with scientists. Similarly, Plato's theory of the state, and particularly his theory of education as a function of the state, has been denounced as Fascist. Plato may have been wrong or we may have misunderstood Plato; but the important fact to note is that these are not crucial to the idealist doctrine of man.

The points that are truly crucial might be listed as follows:

(1) Man is to be understood as in essence nonmaterial. He has commerce with the material world, but he is not a part of it. Thus, the reductive procedure of the materialist is rejected.

(2) Man possesses certain unique faculties that differentiate him from all nonliving things, possibly from the animals. The highest of these is reason. He is thus a rational being.

(3) Since the capacity for reasoning is what permits man to grasp the ideas which constitute the essence of reality, the understanding of man himself must be based on the logical analysis of his experience. An idealistic psychology is likely to be a rigorously deductive system, using the test of logical consistency rather than that of correspondence with observation.

As we shall see, much of Plato's rationalism was absorbed into the later Aristotelian and Christian psychologies. Something akin to a pure Platonism might be recognized as the recurrent attempts to explain the nature of man in terms of formal logical and mathematical models. Such an effort was made in the early 19th century by Herbart (cf. p. 186). More recent examples might be drawn from the factor analysis movement. When, for instance, the psychologist uses statistical tools to identify the "pure" factors in intelligence or personality, he does not pretend that these factors are data of direct observation or that they will ever be directly observed;

they are deduced from observation and tested by logic and mathematics. Yet as the psychologist progressively refines his analysis he believes that he is approaching a series of statements that are true. The factors are not entities in a material world; they are more like Plato's ideas, essential relationships to which the material world conforms.

ARISTOTLE, AND THE TELEOLOGICAL DOCTRINE OF MAN

Aristotle's philosophy is regarded by some scholars as a major alternative to that of Plato, by others as essentially an extension and systematization of Plato's thought. The issue need not concern us here. In the Aristotelian treatment of man, however, we find a central principle which, although present in Plato, is developed with such clarity as to warrant its being labelled an Aristotelian doctrine. This is the teleological principle, in terms of which the understanding of man is to be sought in the implicit purpose which gradually reveals itself in his development. The battle over the status of purpose in scientific explanation always goes back to Aristotle.

Aristotle (384–322 B.C.) was born in Stagira in Macedonia (hence the frequent reference to him as the Stagirite), but most of his productive life was spent in Athens where for nineteen years he was a member of Plato's group in the Academy. Shortly after Plato's death in 347 B.C. he established his own school, the Lyceum, which was destined to become one of the most productive centers of intellectual activity in the history of science. The interests of the Lyceum knew no bounds, and the amount of research accomplished there under Aristotle's leadership was prodigious. Not only did Aristotle explore, and write about, the problems of all the traditional philosophic disciplines; he also systematized and enriched the store of knowledge in all the sciences of nature. His contributions were not all of equal merit, and some, like his astronomical theories, gave false leads; but it is significant that in almost any field of human inquiry, whether it be metaphysics, literary criticism, biology or psychology, the student can with profit "go back and read Aristotle." Aristotle is duller and more difficult reading than Plato, but the rewards justify the effort. For the psychologist the basic source is the *De Anima*

(Concerning the Soul), but Aristotle's psychological theories crop up in many other works as well, notably the *Logic,* the *Ethics,* the *Poetics,* the *Rhetoric,* and even in his work on biology.

Before examining the Aristotelian doctrine of man we must examine briefly his general approach and a few of his basic concepts. Aristotle has sometimes been classed as a Realist, but the meaning of this term has been so confused in its history that it adds little to our understanding. He could with equal correctness be classed as an Idealist, for his philosophy resembles that of Plato more than it does that of many of the modern Realists. Aristotle agreed with Plato in rejecting a simple materialism and in insisting that a final explanation must be in terms of nonmaterial principles. He disagreed with Plato's belief in Ideas as independent existences; for him the Ideas are the forms of material substance, except in the case of God who is Pure Form. Thus the Ideas cannot, except through a process of abstraction, be separated from matter, any more than matter can be conceived, except through abstraction, as an independent existent. The task of the philosopher-scientist is, through the study of formed matter in all its concrete instances, to derive the principles of form (the Ideas). Thus one of the crucial differences between the two lies in the role they accorded to the observation of particular instances. For Plato the particular thing or event can conveniently *illustrate* a principle that unfettered reason can grasp directly without observation; observation of the particular is, as it were, a pedagogical device, an aid to communication. For Aristotle, *the principles reveal themselves through the observation of particulars,* although the principles cannot be formulated except through the operation of reason. The essential difference between Plato and Aristotle is regarded by some as a difference in method.

The Aristotelian method has often been described as the method of deduction of consequences from premises, and so has been contrasted with the inductive method of modern science. This is true of his Logic, in which he set the famous pattern of the syllogism: major premise, minor premise, conclusion.[1] It is not true, however, of his science. The Aristotelian method in science is that of observation, classification, and then deduction of implications. As we shall see

---

[1] All men are mortal;
   Socrates is a man;
   Therefore, Socrates is mortal.

later, the revival of Aristotle's method of induction (cf. p. 101) had much to do with the emergence of the new science in the sixteenth century. Aristotle's inductive method is open to criticism in that he allowed his preconceptions to intervene at the various stages of the inductive process and never worked out adequate empirical tests of his conclusions; for him the test of logical consistency was still sufficient. No scientist, however, has ever been completely invulnerable to such a criticism. Aristotle can still be rightly regarded as the father of Western science.

If we are to understand the Aristotelian doctrine of man, however, we must be clear about the conceptual framework within which he observed, classified and interpreted the phenomena of nature. It is immaterial whether we regard this as a set of preconceptions or as a set of conclusions. To oversimplify, here are some of the main concepts we must keep in mind:

(1) *Matter and form.* Any object exists as a concrete reality in space and time. It is composed of something (matter), but it exists only as something particular (a stone, a tree, a human body) *i.e.,* it is formed matter. Through a process of abstraction one can conceive of formless matter or matterless form, but these are simply conceptions. The reality we know is matter that has form; but form cannot be reduced to terms of matter.

(2) *Potential and actual.* Potential means "what is possible;" actual means "what is." A block of marble is potentially a great number of different statues, but it is not potentially a human being. A human being is potentially a criminal or a saint, but he is not potentially an elephant. In each case the actual form of matter has placed certain restrictions on the number and kind of forms that might be actualized from it. The hypothetical formless matter is potentially anything, since it contains all possible forms. Thus any actual thing contains various potentialities, but the range of these is a function of actual form.

(3) *Inherent properties.* Formed matter has certain properties, but some of these are essential and others accidental. A piece of iron when dropped will fall to the ground rather than float in the air, because iron is inherently heavy. Heavy objects fall and light objects, like balloons, rise. The same piece of iron might be heated or cooled, but its particular temperature is an accident of circumstance. Iron is heavy, but it is not essentially hot or cold. So far as temperature is concerned, the only inescapable fact about iron is that it is capable

of variations. This capacity is inherent in iron, but the particular temperature is an accident. Thus we may distinguish between properties that are inherent and properties that are accidental. If we wish to know the true nature of the object we must identify the properties that are really inherent.

(4) *Causality.* The answer to the question, "Why?", naturally begins with "because." When you release the stone, why does it fall? Because you dropped it? Because it is heavy? Or because of something else? Whatever is followed by the word "because" reveals your theory of causality.

For Aristotle there are four types of cause, all of which participate in every event: the material, the efficient, the formal and the final. Let us consider the familiar billiard ball example. Ball A, struck by the cue, strikes Ball B, and then Ball B moves at the appropriate angle with the appropriate velocity. What causes the movement of Ball B? The efficient cause is clearly the force transmitted from A to B. But we must also consider the material cause. If A were a balloon it would not cause the same movement in B. Then there is a formal cause, the flatness of the table and the roundness of the balls are also important. "On a cloth untrue with a twisted cue and elliptical billiard balls" the result would be quite different. And lastly there is the intent of the billiard player. Assuming that he is a skillful player, he has taken advantage of all the other conditions to produce the desired result. The purpose expressed through the event is the final cause. ("Final" here means "end", not in the sense of "coming to a stop" but in the sense of "goal to be attained." *Cf.* the French adjective *"final"* and the German adjective *"Zweckmässig."*)

Material, formal and efficient causes are all consonant with a materialistic explanation. The materialist explains events in terms of antecedent and concomitant conditions. What Aristotle added was the final cause, the teleological principle without which, he believed, no object or event in nature could be fully explained.

(5) *The teleological principle.* Teleology means the doctrine of ends, or purposes. To be a teleologist is to insist that we cannot understand a thing or an event without reference to the purpose behind it or inherent in it. There are two kinds of teleology, a transcendent and an immanent (indwelling) teleology. The transcendent teleologist believes in a purpose behind events, possibly in a God who has planned in advance all that is to come. Nearly all the

traditional religions have been centered about a transcendent teleology. The immanent teleologist believes that there is an inherent purposiveness within the processes of nature. Nature as a whole, and every process within nature, is directed towards a goal. The distinction between the two types of teleology is not a clear one. Although many transcendent teleologies have not included the assumption of immanent purpose, *e.g.*, as in the early Hebrew theology revealed in the books of Moses, most immanent teleologies imply the existence, or at least the pre-existence, of a transcendent purpose. Thus the religion of modern liberal Protestantism is an immanent teleology, but most Protestant theologians believe in a transcendent God.

Aristotle shared with the enlightened Greeks of his day a belief in a Supreme Being, who embodied the *Summun Bonum* (the Highest Good), who was the First Cause and the Final Cause of all existence. In this sense he was a transcendent teleologist. For us, however, it is Aristotle's immanent teleology that is interesting. He believed that the purposes of the Supreme Being are built into Nature. Every natural object or process has its *entelechy* (inherent purpose) in accordance with which it behaves. It is appropriate that light objects should rise and heavy objects fall, that cats should behave like cats and dogs like dogs, that man if he is to be fully human should exercise his capacity for reasoning.

Aristotle's teleology thus brings into a single focus his distinctions between matter and form, potential and actual, essential and accidental properties, and final causes as contrasted with the other types of cause. Any object is to be regarded as having its own inner nature which is gradually actualized as it comes into being, the discovery of which is the basis of our true understanding of it.

Within this framework Aristotle gives us a consistent interpretation of man. It is true that man is a part of physical nature, *i.e.*, is composed of matter, but the essence of man, the soul, belongs in the category of form. It is something that is gradually actualized during the course of his development. Soul is not to be regarded after the fashion of Plato as something essentially independent of the body; it is rather the formal principle in accordance with which the body operates. Aristotle is accordingly much less convinced than was Plato of the immortality of the soul. He concedes that the rational principle is indestructible, but whether it can survive as a concrete entity is less clear.

In the first chapter of *De Anima,* Aristotle defines the problem of psychology as that of ascertaining "the nature and essence of soul, and its attributes." The essence of soul, we have seen, is that it is a formal principle, the form of organization of the body. But what are its attributes? The attributes of soul can be ascertained only through systematic observation. In his speculation about "essences" Aristotle was carrying on the rational tradition of Plato, a tradition that was to dominate psychological thought for many centuries. In his search for "attributes" he was launching the empirical movement in psychology. Rational psychology is concerned with the origin, the nature and the destiny of the soul. Empirical psychology is concerned with the observation, classification and interpretation of the manifestations of soul in human experience and behavior. For Aristotle both kinds of psychology were legitimate, but, as we shall see, the empirical movement in psychology was not revived until long after the rebirth of science in the sixteenth century. Aristotle's empirical findings were frozen into a rational pattern, and his spirit of empirical inquiry was lost.

In his observation of human behavior, Aristotle was impressed by the continuity between man and other forms of life. He did not have the modern conception of biological evolution, but he recognized man as an advanced product of a developmental process. Beginning with hypothetical formless matter, evolution gives us in progressive stages a movement upward in the direction of pure form, with rationality at the apex. Commentators have frequently attributed to Aristotle the conception of three souls: the nutritive, common to all living things, the sensitive, common to animals and man, and the rational, unique to man. Here the word "soul" is somewhat misleading, however. What he was emphasizing was that there are different modes of organization of matter, each with its own potentialities and its own entelechies. Inanimate things possess extension, weight, hardness and so forth, but they cannot grow and reproduce. Plants are organized in such a way that they grow and reproduce (the nutritive principle), but they have no sensation and no voluntary movement. Animals are governed by the nutritive principle, and they are also capable of perception and voluntary motion (the sensitive principle), but they cannot think rationally. Man is unique in that he is capable of rational thought. Aristotle's language suggests a radical cleft between man and the animals, and subsequent interpreters of

Aristotle have raised this to the level of dogma. It is true that Aristotle was so impressed by the uniqueness of man's rationality that he conceived of man as having a unique kind of soul. The whole purport of his argument, however, is that in successive stages of evolution more and more potentialities become actual. Evolution is a striving upward toward the ultimate goal of rationality. Each individual and each species strives toward the actualization of its own potentiality, but each particular actualization is to be regarded as part of a larger pattern.

Acceptance of the teleological principle means that if we are to understand man or animal, or even any human or animal structures like arms and eyes and brains, we cannot be content with the discovery of the material, the efficient, or even the formal, causes; we must discover the inherent purpose of each structure, the part it plays in the total plan. We learn something about the eye, for instance, by dissecting it, by observing the reflexes of the pupil and by studying the transmission of light to the retina, but we have not fully understood the eye until we realize that it is, in the naive language of a child, "something to see with." Hands are "to grasp with". The brain, Aristotle wrongly concluded, serves the purpose of correcting excess heat, but he might well have anticipated Galen and regarded it as "something to think with." Material and efficient causes may account for individual differences, but only the final cause can give us a complete explanation. The structures of any animal are designed to enable it most efficiently to grow, to reproduce, and to react (perception and locomotion) to the objects in its environment. The constitution of man is designed to serve these simple purposes, but it is also designed to enable man to attain the higher goal of the Good Life.

Thus the inherent purpose of any object is to behave in accordance with its own inner nature. Just as a ship that is too long and narrow to maintain stability is not a proper ship, and a horse that has lost one of its limbs is not a proper horse, so a man whose conduct is not guided by reason is not behaving as a proper man. The task of the scientist is to gain an understanding of the inner nature of things, to observe particular structures and processes and to show how they play a part in fulfilling general purposes.

What then are the essential structures and purposes of man? Aristotle's analysis is too rich and detailed to be presented here.

Essentially, man is an animal, but he is a *rational* animal. As an animal he possesses the structures necessary for growth, reproduction, perception and locomotion. His animal nature provides him with appetites which, as Plato has pointed out, must be kept under control; with senses which enable him to respond to the world about him; with mobility which permits him to escape danger and pursue his goals. As a rational being he behaves within the context of his animal nature, but he is able to transcend it. Reason, however, cannot operate by itself; it must make use of what is furnished by the lower faculties. The laws of pure reason are to be found in the discipline of Logic, but reasoning as it actually takes place is clouded by perception, memory and imagination. Hence Aristotle's interest in the lower faculties.

Aristotle's study of the processes of cognition gave us a theory, possibly wrong but beautifully simple, which has appealed to psychologists ever since. The basis is the doctrine of the senses. There are five senses, the gateways of the mind: vision, audition, taste, smell and touch, which give us the five basic qualities out of which all experience is constructed. There is no "sixth" sense. There is, however, a *sensus communis,* a second-order common sense that integrates the data of the individual senses into percepts; and there are the capacities of memory and imagination which permit us to retain and recombine the data of the several senses and preserve them as ideas. There are furthermore the principles of association: similarity, contrast and contiguity of space and time, which account for the fact that one idea can suggest another. Thus, even before reason enters in, we find that mental life, like physical nature, is behaving in accordance with law. Sensations, percepts and ideas are phenomena of nature that can be studied as such and that can form the basis of a science. This is perhaps Aristotle's greatest contribution to the scientific study of man.

The rational principle, however, was for Aristotle something to be derived not from observation but from logical deduction, and the laws of thinking are accordingly the laws of logic. Knowledge has as its content the data of the senses, organized and interpreted by reason. The central faculty of reason is thus the only faculty of the soul that can apprehend pure form, *i.e.,* can abstract form from its material setting, and can consequently know truth. In his treatment of reason Aristotle follows in the footsteps of his teacher Plato. Even today psychologists still find it difficult to disentangle the empirical psychology of thinking from the formal categories of logic.

We shall see that Aristotle's distinction between peripheral sensory processes and central intellective processes has played an important role in the history of cognitive theory. The assumption is that certain elementary data (givens) are provided by the senses and that these are then reworked by the mind. The persistent question is: How much of knowledge comes from the senses, and how much from the mind?

THE RELIGIOUS DOCTRINE OF MAN

It is with some hesitation that one speaks of *the* religious doctrine of man. The religions of the world have been so varied in their beliefs and their practices that one sometimes despairs of finding any common characteristics. Nevertheless each religion has contained an implicit doctrine of man, and one is tempted to believe that all religions, from the most "primitive" to the most "emancipated", have enough in common to distinguish their doctrine of man from the nonreligious doctrines. Religion will here be identified as an attitude which involves: (1) a belief in an order of reality that transcends the material, which may or may not be personified as a deity; (2) a feeling of reverence (self-abasement or possibly only fear) with respect to the transcendent order; and (3) the acceptance of certain obligations upon personal conduct, which may be merely constraints. Religions have differed in their relative emphasis on these three components, some stressing theology, others ritual and still others ethics, but all three are present to some extent in every religion. From the religious point of view man must be considered as something apart from the natural order of things; or else, nature must be reinterpreted in terms other than those of conventional science.

Both Plato and Aristotle might, according to these criteria, be considered as exponents of a religious doctrine and, as we shall see, some of the teachings of both were absorbed into Christian theology. Their doctrines, however, were essentially rationalistic. Although God, as in Aristotle, might be identified as Pure Reason, neither

Plato nor Aristotle believed that the understanding of man required the assumption of supernatural laws. The best examples of the religious doctrine of man are to be found in the religions of the Middle East and the Far East. For our present purpose, the Hebraic-Christian tradition will have to suffice.

After Aristotle's death in 322 B.C. the scientific productivity of Athens began to decline. Alexander's conquests had spread Greek influence far and wide, but with Alexander's death in 323 B.C. the controlling hand was lost. Greek culture persisted, in Asia Minor, in Alexandria, in Southern Italy, but the fountainhead was stopped. The passionate curiosity about facts that had been embodied in the Lyceum degenerated into gentle speculation about the ends of human existence. The Stoics and the Epicureans had much of importance to say about the theory of human motivation, and the Stoics in particular exercised considerable influence on early Christian theology, but there is nothing in their doctrines that was not to be found, better stated, in Socrates, Plato and Aristotle. In Asia Minor the Greek language persisted as the language of culture. In Alexandria there was a productive cross-fertilization of Greek and Hebrew scholarship which had much to do with the later development of Christian theology. In Sicily and Southern Italy the Greek colonies produced scientists of high caliber, like Archimedes (287–212 B.C.), whose discoveries were to herald the new science that was to come many centuries later. But the Greek emphasis on the intellectual, persistent though it proved to be, was destined to be temporarily overwhelmed by militant religion.

The religion of the West is rooted in the Hebraic tradition. The Hebrews are, by legend, a Mesopotamian tribe who migrated westward, spent some time in Egypt, returned to conquer the land between the Jordan and the Mediterranean coast, set up a flourishing kingdom, which resisted numerous invasions and which finally crumbled before the power of the Romans. Their great contribution is a monotheistic religion and a strict ethical code. Yahweh, originally a tribal god, petulant, irascible and unpredictable, gradually grew in their conception to the status of a Universal God who demanded right thinking and right conduct from all people, regardless of race or nation. The doctrine of man implicit in the ancient Hebrew tradition is far from consistent, but at least it gives us a picture of man as a creature who is free to choose between right and wrong, *i.e.*, between obedience to the will of his god, which will be rewarded, and disobedience, which will be punished. True, Yahweh frequently "hardened the hearts" of certain people so that they might be punished for their sins, thereby demonstrating the greatness of Yahweh; but, as contrasted with the fatalism of the Greek religions, which allowed no room for voluntary deviation from the plans of the gods (cf. the legend of Oedipus), the Hebrew conception is of man as a free spirit. Whereas the Greek philosophers paid little more than lip service to their religion, and Greek rationalism is consequently at bottom an alternative to, rather than an interpretation of, the current religious doctrines, the thinking of the Hebrew prophets was centered about the implications for conduct of an unchallenged religious faith. There was no room in the Hebrew tradition for the kind of free speculation that secured for Athens its unique place in intellectual history, for to think freely would be a denial of faith. The Hebrews consequently gave us no great philosophic systems. Nevertheless, the Hebrew faith in God, when combined with the Greek faith in reason, was destined to give us an elaborate philosophy which included a clear and consistent doctrine of man.

The Christian doctrine of man was first formulated by Paul (d.ca. 67 A.D.). Paul's heritage and education included the culture of both the Hebrews and the Greeks, and he was by birth a Roman citizen. His conversion to Christianity, *i.e.,* to the belief that Jesus of Nazareth was God's Anointed, was sudden and dramatic. Thereafter he tirelessly traveled the countries of the Eastern Mediterranean, establishing Christian communities, and was later transported to Rome for trial as a troublemaker where, exonerated, he laid the foundations of the Roman church and where eventually he died. Paul was an organizing genius, but he was also a penetrating thinker who, fired with the idealism of Hebrew faith, yet shared the Greek passion for an explanation of things. Although he did not give us a philosophic system, he gives us an approach that differs quite markedly from that of the Greeks.

Paul's religion is a religion *about* Jesus, not to be confused with the religion *of* Jesus. Jesus (ca. 4 B.C.–ca. 33 A.D.) belongs in the tradition of the Hebrew prophets who believed that they had a mission from God to save their people. Jesus may have conceived of himself as unique, as the promised Messiah (deliverer) of his people, but his conception of the messianic role was clearly not that of the conqueror of enemies or the rebuilder of temples. For him, deliverance (salvation) was the result of an inner act of self-dedication to the will of God. "He that loseth his life, will save it."

The Jesus of History may never be recovered. For Paul, however, who had had no personal contact with Jesus, the person was less important than the symbol. Jesus, the Christ, was the symbol of man's potential regeneration. "Believe in the Lord Jesus Christ and thou shalt be saved." The principles of living which Jesus taught, and which are embedded in the Hebrew tradition, became an essential part of the new Christian religion; but, in addition to right living, Paul demanded a belief in the unique status of Jesus as the Christ, *i.e.,* he was laying the groundwork of a new theology. In the subsequent history of Christianity the ethical and religious concerns of Jesus have frequently been lost in theological debate.

The Christian doctrine of man must consequently be understood in the context of Christian theology. For the early Christians the ultimate reality is God, the creator of the universe, the shaper of man's destiny. God is a spirit, transcending space and time, omniscient, omnipresent and omnipotent. Man is also a spirit, *i.e.,* he contains within him a spark of the divine, but he is a spirit enclosed within a mortal body. Only as he conquers the weaknesses of the flesh is he able to achieve full communion with God and attain his true end which, in the words of the Shorter Catechism is "to glorify God and enjoy him forever." The Christians accepted literally the Hebrew legend of man's fall from a state of grace into a state of sin, and interpreted the history both of the individual and of the race as the upward striving of man towards the re-establishment of unity (atonement) with God. To this the Christians added the conception of the Christ as the intermediary between God and man, through whose sacrifice man's salvation is rendered possible.

The early Christian doctrine obviously has much in common with that of Plato; but there is an important difference. Both Plato and Paul regard the life of man as a battle between the forces of his higher and his lower nature, and for the Christians this battle became a grim life-and-death affair dramatized as a struggle for the soul of man between God and the Devil. Both the Greeks and the Christians are agreed that man's lower nature is revealed in his impulses and appetites. (For the Christians the sexual impulse gradually became the prime symbol of evil, although by some extremists even the enjoyment of food and of bodily comfort were regarded as sinful.) Both the Greeks and the Christians believed that if man is to achieve the Good Life he must conquer his lower nature. Characteristically, however, for the Greeks (Socrates) wisdom must be preceded by a conviction of ignorance; for the Christians (Paul), salvation must be preceded by a conviction of sin.

It is in the interpretation of man's Higher Nature, however, that we find the most important difference. For the Greeks the Good Life is the life governed by Reason. Socrates argues that knowledge and virtue are one, that moral problems can be solved only by clear thinking. Plato recognized the "spirited element" in man, but held that it should support but not control man's reason. In Aristotle's system the capacity for reasoning was unique to man. In the Christian doctrine of man Plato's "spirited element" is broadened in its conception to include the Hebrew notion of Spirit, and it is promoted to a position above that of Reason. Reason alone cannot secure salvation; it must be Reason governed by Faith. Faith is the nonrational orientation of the whole individual towards the true and the good, *i.e.*, towards God. In more modern language, to have faith is to bet one's life on the reality of certain values, the validity of which requires no rational demonstration. *Credo ut intelligam.* One cannot fully understand unless one first believes.

The Christian doctrine of man is thus an extension, but also an inversion, of the Platonic doctrine. Man is an immaterial and immortal entity, dependent not on his own rational powers but on his God for all that he is to achieve. The secret of the Good Life is not merely clear thinking but right willing. The individual who has accepted the will of God will know what is true and will be guided to what is right. This is a transcendent teleology. There is a natural order, but above and beyond it there is a supernatural order which gives direction to the natural. Man can have absolute knowledge of what is true and what is good only when this has been revealed by the supernatural being.

The subsequent history of the Christian doctrine of man is the history of Christian theology, and this is confused by the history of the Christian Church. As the centuries went by the Church grew from a scattering of small, devoted and regularly persecuted communities, mostly of lower and lower-middle socio-economic class, to an organization of great political and even military power that helped to shape the destiny of Western Europe. (By the 4th century, Christendom had acquired in Constantine its first Christian Roman emperor). The struggles within the Church had to do with doctrine, with policy and with power, and some of these led to wars as brutal and as senseless as any that have disgraced the history of mankind. Much of Christian history bears little relevance to the religion of Jesus, nor even to that of Paul.

Nevertheless, the fifteen centuries that succeeded Paul bear witness to the persistent and passionate effort on the part of Christian theologians to clarify their thinking about the nature of man and his relation to God. Paul, as we have seen, was a child of both the Hebrews and the Greeks. As the architect of Christian doctrine he drew on both traditions. But there were certain inconsistencies that he never succeeded in resolving. Most of these were theological, which we cannot consider here. So far as the doctrine of man is concerned, however, there were two great unsolved problems: (1) the problem of human freedom, and (2) the relation between faith and reason, i.e., the problem of revelation. Neither has ever been finally answered, but two of the noblest attempts are to be found in the writings of Augustine and Thomas Aquinas, the former a Platonist, the latter an Aristotelian.

Augustine (354–430), Bishop of Hippo in North Africa, lived during the twilight of the Roman Empire, and died as the Vandals were completing their conquest of the Roman territories in North Africa. An early deviate from Christianity, and for many years an active opponent, he was eventually reconverted and rose to a position of eminence in the Church. He was a capable organizer, a skillful debater, a relentless persecutor of heresy, and a theologian of great stature. Many historians regard him as the bridge between the Classical Greek and the Scholastic periods. At any rate, he was for a thousand years one of the dominant influences in Western thought and did more than any other to fuse the Idealism of Plato with the religious fervor of Paul into a consistent Christian theology.

In the writings of Augustine, notably the *Confessions* and the *City of God,* we have perhaps the best expression of the religious doctrine of man. The only reality is spiritual. The Idea of Good (in Plato's sense) is the Supreme Spirit, or God. God created the universe in accordance with a plan, and in doing so endowed man with the potentiality of knowing with certainty that which is true. The process is that of observing one's own experience. God has implanted in us ideas of the eternal which, if we are disciplined by faith, we can recognize. Mere observation of nature (science) gives a knowledge of temporal things, but knowledge of the eternal can result only from "divine illumination." Since God is the sole creator, and man but a partial expression of God's will, it follows that man can *learn* from the study of nature but can *know with certainty* only through divine revelation. Science is thus disparaged as interesting but inconsequential, useful for the conduct of practical affairs, but irrelevant to the solution of man's deepest problem which is to attain salvation.

Augustine accepted Plato's solution of the mind-body relationship. The cognitive problem disappeared once the principle of divine revelation was accepted. The aesthetic experience became a by-product of the relation of man to God; contemplation of the divine fills one with the ecstasy of love. It was the problem of Will that resisted solution, and that has plagued all theologians before and since. If God created the universe, and is thereby responsible for all that is, how can man be considered as responsible for his actions? The problem crops up in Greek mythology and in Hebrew legend, but no adequate solution is offered. The later Hebrew prophets, and Paul, inclined towards a belief in the freedom of human choice, but they never resolved the evident inconsistency of such a belief with their theology. Augustine, spurred by his study of the Greek rationalists, wrestled with the problem, and also failed. In his earlier years he apparently favored a doctrine of freedom. As he became more and more embroiled in the controversies of the church and in the refutation of heresies he seems to have moved in the direction of determinism. At any rate with Augustine the problem comes into clear focus. Either man is free to make choices or, pushing the Christian theology to its full implication, man's fate is completely predestined. The controversy was to rage for many centuries both in the Roman Catholic and later in the Protestant churches, and in modern science the problem emerges again as the alternative between determinism and indeterminacy.

Quite apart from his significance for religion and theology Augustine is to be recognized as one of the great expositors of what was to become a fundamental method of psychology, namely the meticulous observation of one's own consciousness. Socrates had stressed the importance of self-knowledge, and all the Greeks who succeeded him drew upon the evidence of self-observation. For Aristotle, however, the study of nature was an equally important source of truth. In the Augustinian system there is no place for science as we now understand the term. Truth can be realized only through the discovery in one's own consciousness of what God has planted there. The introspective method exemplified by Augustine's *Confessions* is far from the "dispassionate" inspection of experience advocated by the modern phenomenologists, for Augustine in his introspection was passionately searching for God. Whatever the motive, however, we find in Augustine's scrutiny of his own experience an approach which was later to become explicit in the writings of Descartes, Husserl and even Sartre.

Augustine gave us a Christianized version of Plato. He had read some of Aristotle's works, but he was not challenged by Aristotle's interest in nature. For him the revelation of God through human experience was completely convincing and satisfying. During the succeeding centuries, as the Church grew in size and power, the Christian theologians were forced to grapple more realistically with the problems of Nature and of Society. By the tenth century the Church was a political entity. It owned vast properties. Its Pope could make or break a dynasty. Its priests could control the thoughts and feelings of the humblest citizens. The Church was the repository of learning, the dictator of morals, the sponsor of wars against the heathen. It is understandable that the theologians should have turned from Plato to Aristotle; for Aristotle was a more "down to earth" philosopher. Aristotle looked at Nature and Society and found a meaningful pattern, and this pattern seemed to be quite consistent with the transcendent teleology of Christianity. During the Middle Ages the works of Aristotle, in their Latin version, became almost as authoritative as the sacred writings of the Bible.

The period of the Middle Ages is a convenient fiction of the historian, representing a dark stretch in the history of Europe between an idealized "ancient" and an equally idealized "modern" period. It was "dark" in the sense that it was relatively unknown until fairly recent times and that it lacked the glitter of Ancient Greece. It was not, however, a period of somnolence. It witnessed the growth and the crumbling of empires, the continuous struggles for supremacy among feudal, and eventually national, powers, the westward march of Islam, the repeated attempts of western adventurers to liberate the Holy Land from the "infidels," and the slow movement of western culture to the northern European cities. In the context of the history of ideas it witnessed the steady consolidation of Christian doctrine. As the Church gained in political power it won battle after battle against the heresies that threatened its theology, and at the same time it struggled from within to clarify its own principles. There were controversies over the wording of the creed, over the conception of the trinity, over the reality of Ideas, the "Realists" contending that Ideas are real entities, the "Nominalists" holding that they are merely arbitrary classifications, and over many other problems. But the big puzzle was how to reconcile the conflicting doctrines of Faith and Reason, and this was what Thomas Aquinas attempted to do.

Thomas Aquinas (1225–74) was a towering figure in mediaeval scholarship, and is generally regarded as the greatest of the Christian interpreters of Aristotle. Reformulated by the modern Neo-Thomists to take into account the subsequent centuries of scientific discovery, the Thomistic system may now be accepted as the basic philosophy of orthodox Roman Catholicism. Today the Roman Catholic student of psychology is likely to be introduced to the subject by way of Part I of the *Summa Theologica,* or at least by way of a textbook based on this work.

Born near Naples, Thomas Aquinas early came under the influence of the Dominican scholar Albertus Magnus, and spent most of his active life as a teacher in Paris. His vast scholarship, his penetrating logic and his tireless devotion pushed him quickly into a position of leadership in the Church's struggle for a clarification of its doctrine. We have noted that Christian doctrine had come to rest more and more on Aristotle; but the editions of Aristotle's works were incomplete and unreliably translated into Latin. The Aristotle whom the Christians knew and revered was definitely Christianized. It consequently came as a shock to the theologians when, in the twelfth century, new translations and even new Aristotelian works began to appear. What had been accepted as dogma was now being challenged. This challenge came in part from the Arabs.

During the centuries since Augustine the new religion of Islam had come into being. Initiated, as in the case of Christianity, by a man with a deep conviction of religious mission, the religion became a powerful movement, and the man Mohammed (ca. 570–632) became enshrouded in legend. Islam is a monotheistic religion, claiming the best in the Hebrew and Christian traditions, but insisting that the final prophetic revelation came through Mohammed. Like the religion of the Hebrews it stressed ritualistic observance and moral rectitude; like Christianity it became vigorously evangelical. Unlike Christianity, it rejected the doctrine of the total depravity of man. Shortly after the death of Mohammed the Arab Muslims (believers in Islam) began, partly by military conquest and partly by peaceful penetration, to spread their influence. In a hundred years they were in control of most of what is now the Middle East, had spread westward across North Africa, had conquered Spain, and had even invaded Southern France. During the succeeding centuries they consolidated one of the great civilizations of human history. By the twelfth century they were regarded by Christian Europe as the Great Enemy against whom religious Crusades should be launched.

The Arabs in their westward movement brought a culture of their own, traces of which are easily recognized in the architecture, the painting and the languages of Western Europe. They also brought different versions of the science and philosophy of the Greeks. The Arabs had maintained, for instance, a lively interest in the medical sciences and in mathematics, and they had preserved their own records of Aristotle's writings, some of which were unknown to the Christian scholars. When the great Arabic-Spanish scholar Averroës (1126–1198) began to circulate his commentaries on Aristotle, the orthodox Christian interpretation seemed to some to have been undermined. What came to be known as Averroism was interpreted rightly or wrongly as a denial of the Christian doctrine of personal immortality and an assertion that there are two different realms of truth, Faith and Reason, which do not necessarily coincide. For a brief period the study of Aristotle was actually banned at the University of Paris.

It was Thomas Aquinas who, more than anyone else, succeeded in resolving the conflict and in re-establishing Aristotle as the philosopher of Christianity. The theological issues which he dissected and clarified are beyond the scope of our present inquiry. What is of greatest importance to us as psychologists is the relation between Faith and Reason. The Greeks had exalted Reason as the secret of the Good Life. The Early Christians made Reason subservient to Faith. For the Mediaeval Christians the problem of reconciling the two was the great challenge. In the system of Thomas Aquinas we have a defense of Faith *through* Reason, a rational doctrine of man that incorporates a belief in God, in the immortality of the human soul and in the freedom of man to choose between right and wrong. Whether or not we accept such a doctrine we must respect its clarity and consistency.

The Thomistic psychology is Aristotelian in all except its presuppositions and its conclusions. It presupposes a God whose purposes are being actualized in the lives of men, and it concludes that the nature and purposes of God can be rationally derived through the scrutiny of man's experience. It is thus both a transcendent and an immanent teleology. Its specific answers to the persistent psychological questions are little more than elaborations of what we have already found in Aristotle. The human soul possesses three sets of faculties, the organic, the sensory and the rational. The organic faculties, as in Aristotle, include those of generation, nutrition and growth. There are three classes of sensory faculty, the sensory-cognitive, the sensory-orectic (appetitive) and the motor. Under the sensory-cognitive we have the traditional five senses, plus the more general faculties of perception (*sensus cummunis*), imagination, judgment and memory. The sensory-orectic faculties are responsible for the appetites of man's lower nature which enable him to survive and reproduce, and the motor faculty is similarly the power of locomotion.

The organic and sensory faculties are parts of man's lower nature, and operate in and through the body. There is thus a legitimate place in the Thomistic psychology for the study of the physical and physiological aspects of mental life. The rational faculties, on the other hand, do not depend on the body, and cannot be understood through the procedures of natural science. There are two types of rational faculty, intellect and will. Intellect, which may be active or passive, contains the power of reasoning and understanding. Will, which is sometimes called "intellectual appetite" is the principle in man that actively directs him towards the knowledge of God. We have here the Thomistic reconciliation of Faith and Reason. Will and intellect are co-ordinate powers of a single rational soul. The proper approach to God is not through the denial of Reason but through the full use of one's rational powers. The revelation of God to man is fullest when man thinks most actively and most clearly.

The Thomistic psychology is thus rationalistic, in the Greek sense, but at the same time fundamentally religious. It provides an orderly account of the capacities and tendencies inherent in man, and it leaves room for an empirical science that describes, classifies and, in a limited sense, explains the relation between mind and body, the basis of cognition and the basis of conduct; but it holds stubbornly to the belief that in his essence man is not a member of the natural order and must be understood ultimately in terms not of natural but of spiritual law.

The system of Thomas Aquinas did not settle the controversies of the Church, nor did it receive immediate wide acceptance. Although it restored Aristotle to a position of respectability, its immediate effect was to encourage an uncreative kind of scholarship, overly concerned with minute textual criticisms and fine logical distinctions, that was to make the term "scholastic" almost as opprobrious as that of "sophist." It was not, in fact, until the late nineteenth century that the real power of the Thomistic system began to be appreciated. The term "scholastic" was originally used with reference to the great mediaeval schools of theology, like those at Paris, Chartres and Rheims, but it gradually came to represent a method. The Scholastic method usually involved the presentation of a thesis, *i.e.,* a proposition the truth or falsity of which was to be determined, an orderly listing of all the implications of the thesis in the form of more specific propositions or questions, a careful examination of each of these with an answering of the objections, and a final statement of the true position. Much of the Scholastic writing takes this form, as does the Scholastic pattern of oral debate. The method is clearly a magnificient instrument for the clarification of principles and their implications, and for training in the art of debate. As with any other method, it involves the danger that the technique of inquiry may become so fascinating as to obscure its purpose. The records of the Scholastic period indicate that many of the debates degenerated into unproductive quibbles, concerned more with the defense of a position than with the discovery of truth. Critics of Scholasticism are fond of citing the, possibly legendary, debate over the number of angels that can dance on the head of a pin. Much of the criticism is unfair, but we must recognize the fact that the Scholastics, while achieving a new refinement of the Aristotelian method of logical-deductive analysis, had lost Aristotle's passion for observation. The spirit of the Middle Ages was opposed to empirical science.

RECAPITULATION

We have completed our review of five classic doctrines of man that have come down to us from the early speculations of the philosophers. None can be considered a fully scientific doctrine, in the modern sense of the term "science," in that they lacked the discipline that we now consider essential to the scientific method. They did represent, however, sincere attempts to solve the persistent problems that arise when one wonders about the nature and the attributes of man.

To recapitulate, we have:

(1) *A Relativistic Doctrine* which, denying any absolutes, regards man as an accident of circumstance, possessing no intrinsic properties, capable of limitless variation;

(2) *A Materialistic Doctrine* which regards man as a part of physical nature, to be explained ultimately in terms of physical law;

(3) *An Idealistic Doctrine* which sees in man the temporary actualization of an ideal rational order;

(4) *A Teleological Doctrine* which finds in man an inherent nature, intelligible only in terms of an immanent purpose which reveals itself in his behavior;

(5) *A Religious Doctrine* which regards man as primarily a spiritual being, not exclusively a part of the natural order, not to be understood solely in terms of natural law.

These doctrines are not mutually exclusive. We might simplify by opposing the religious to the non-religious, the materialistic to the non-materialistic, the relativistic to the absolutistic. We might also cluster together the idealistic, the teleological and the religious doctrines, as they were in fact clustered in the system of Thomas Aquinas; or we might hark back to the Realist-Nominalist controversy and argue, with the Nominalists, that classifications are always arbitrary. What is important, however, is not the particular list of doctrines, nor the men who have been used as their illustrations, but the historical fact that man in his quest for an understanding of himself has at different times seen the problem in different ways, considered different data as relevant, used different methods, and accepted different constructs as explanatory. As we pursue the story of man's thinking about man we shall see, in the perspective of history, that the implicit assumptions of the psychologist are fully as important as are his explicit assertions.

PART II

The Renaissance and Its Implications

3

The Meaning

of the Renaissance

THE BACKGROUND OF THE SIXTEENTH CENTURY

THE YEAR 1500 is as convenient as any date to indicate the beginning of the period known as the Renaissance. The Rebirth, like any mammalian birth, represented a slow process of gestation, followed by some fairly rapid and dramatic developments. Unlike the mammalian analogue, however, there was no one moment in time at which the liberation of a new life could be observed. It was only gradually, during the sixteenth, seventeenth and eighteenth centuries that freedom of inquiry became established and that the ideal of a free science began to replace the traditional respect for authority. Subsequent history has amply demonstrated that the ideal of freedom has never at any time been fully achieved.

The metaphor of the Rebirth suggests that freedom had been born and had flourished during the time of the Greeks, that it had subsequently died, and that it was now being reborn. We have seen that in truth the eighteen centuries that succeeded the death of Aristotle, or even the thirteen centuries that succeeded Galen, did witness a considerable restriction of man's freedom to investigate and to think. The Authorities were elevated to an un-challengeable position, and it took a courageous spirit indeed to deviate in any significant way from the rules laid down by Authority. Nevertheless, within the framework permitted, there was no cessation of life. The bitter controversies with which the Church was driven, the endless debates over major and minor points of doctrine, the painstaking commentaries on the classics, and the commentaries on the commentaries, all served to sharpen the dialectic tool and to render explicit both the basic assumptions and the internal logic of the doctrine that was gradually being hammered into shape. In consequence we have in the Christian doctrine of man the most consistent as well as the most elaborate psychological system that has ever been worked out. It is not astonishing that the period of the Renaissance brought no revolution in psychological theory analogous to the revolution that was to take place in man's view of the physical universe. Nor is it astonishing that, although subsequent centuries have witnessed the revival of alternative doctrines of man, the superstructure of Christian psychology has never been demolished. It still stands as a way of understanding man which, if its basic assumptions be accepted, is virtually invulnerable.

At the beginning of the Sixteenth century in Western Europe the orthodox Christian view of the world was completely dominant. The works of Aristotle, edited and reinterpreted to meet the requirements of Christian theology, provided the authoritative interpretation of the world from which no man dared deviate in any radical way. For the orthodox Christian the final word had been said. The scientist who persisted in making new observations was permitted to report them only if he could demonstrate that they in no way weakened the foundation of fundamental doctrine. Conclusions that pointed in a different direction were condemned as heresies, which might be rewarded by torture and even death. For the most part, consequently, we find the new ideas of the sixteenth century appearing in subtly disguised form, circulated privately among colleagues who were known to be liberal, or, as in the case of Copernicus, carefully withheld from publication until after the death of the author.

Nevertheless, the ferment had begun. By the turn of the century conditions were ripe for a new liberation of the human spirit, and courageous men were girding their loins for new adventure. Let us glance briefly at the background of the Renaissance.

(1) The world was rapidly growing larger. Adventurers like Marco Polo (1254–1323) had brought back entrancing stories from remote parts of the world. Portuguese explorers had skirted the African coast, penetrated the dark continent at many points and established

colonies on the islands of the Atlantic and Indian oceans. The New World, discovered first by the Vikings, had been rediscovered by Christopher Columbus (1492) and John Cabot (1497). Magellan's circumnavigation of the globe was to be completed a few years later (1522). People could no longer think in terms of a tight little Mediterranean culture. The world was immense. There were blank spaces in the sixteenth century maps, sometimes containing captions like "Here be monsters"; but the gaps were an invitation to exploration. The sixteenth century invited men to seek new realms to discover and conquer.

(2) Nations were being born. England, France, Spain and Portugal, riven though they were by internal dissension, were emerging from the feudal period and were achieving a new national self-consciousness. Italy was still a cluster of city states, but the political power of the Church was already on the wane and the city states were beginning to behave as nations. The Holy Roman Empire, while still a nominal empire, was crumbling at the edges, leaving a cluster of states that were eventually to become Germany. To be a Nationalist was at that time to have a vision of a new and larger allegiance.

(3) National languages and literatures were coming into being. English, a bastard offspring of Anglo-Saxon and Norman French, had already produced its Chaucer and was shortly to produce its Shakespeare. French had yielded a Francois Villon and was about to foster a Rabelais. Spain's Cervantes was in the making. German was settling down to be a language, as were the Germanic dialects that were eventually to become Dutch and Flemish; and mediaeval Latin was steadily shaping itself into what is now Italian. Of universal importance is the fact that poets, novelists and even some scientists were now writing in the vernacular, and taking pride in the mastery of their medium.

(4) Scholarship was becoming secularized, and the scholarly community was growing in size. Although the clerical influence was still powerful, scholarship was no longer exclusively under the control of the church, and the proportion of nonclerical scholars was rapidly increasing. New universities were being founded all over Europe, many of these under state rather than church auspices. Scholarly interests were extending beyond the traditional professional subjects, theology, law and medicine, to include literature and the sciences.

The new Humanistic movement, typified by the Dutch Erasmus (1467–1536), demanded a broadening and deepening of education to include all subjects that are of vital human concern. The printing press had become an adjunct to scholarship, permitting scholars to examine each other's works and thereby facilitating criticism and counter-criticism. Since Latin was still the official language of scholarship, the boundaries of nationality were not yet barriers to communication.

(5) The grip of the Church was beginning to weaken. Its political and military power had been greatly reduced. Nations and city states might still owe nominal allegiance to Rome, but the Church's method of control had to be that of persuasion and political pressure rather than force. Religion was still a potent factor in the lives of people, whom the threat of excommunication or damnation could still paralyze with fear, but it was no longer self-evident that salvation could be attained only through the agency of a single religious institution. There were stirrings of discontent within the church. Many devout Christians were disturbed by evidences of clerical immorality and corruption, particularly in connection with the selling of "indulgences". When in 1517 Luther nailed his 95 theses to the door of the castle church in Wittenberg he was in no sense challenging Christian principles; he was protesting against what he believed to be unchristian practices.

Martin Luther (1483–1546), an Augustinian priest, a biblical scholar, and a man of boundless energy and courage, is regarded as the initiator of the "reformation." His initial protest was a demand for reform within the church, which was vigorously resisted. After his excommunication in 1520 the protest grew into a new religious movement, Protestantism, which denied the authority of the Pope and asserted the right of the individual to interpret the Bible for himself. Luther was the accepted leader of the new movement, guided it through its doctrinal and procedural battles, and gave it a written authority in his translation of the Bible into the vernacular German. The new Protestant theology, in many ways a hark back to Augustine, was systematized by the French reformer, Jean Calvin (1509–64), who eventually made Geneva the capital city of Protestantism, and by the Scottish John Knox (1505?–1572), who succeeded in making Protestantism an official religion.

The new Protestantism was a grim and austere religion, demanding from its adherents even more self-discipline than had ever been required by the Roman church. Protestants could not escape the consequences of sin through penance and absolution; if they sinned they had to suffer the penalty, which might be eternal damnation. And, furthermore, they had the doctrine of election (predestination). A person might be "elected" to salvation or to damnation; and he had no control over it. The Protestant religion became, in some respects, even more constricting than had that of Roman Catholicism.

In other respects, however, Protestantism was a liberating influence. Protestants were challengers of authority—the authority of the Pope, the authority of Aristotle, the authority of Galen. Just as Luther, with his firm belief in the divine inspiration of the Bible, could exhort his followers to read the Bible and draw their own conclusions, so could other Protestants exhort their followers to look at Nature (as Aristotle had done) and draw their own conclusions. Protestantism in religion was a partial expression of the sixteenth century impulse to look at the world and see what it can teach.

The sixteenth century was thus, in a real sense, a rebirth. There was an ever-broadening world to look at and wonder about; and the observer was being freed of the restrictions—conceptual, religious, political—that had hampered him. The sixteenth century scientist was still terrorized by the Church, confused in his religious beliefs, worried about his livelihood—but entranced by the new world that was opening up.

The new developments in the sciences were so dramatic and far reaching in their implications as to merit the term revolutionary. In a scant two hundred years the whole picture of the universe was radically altered, and all the old Greek questions about the nature of man and his place in the universe arose anew, demanding reformulation in the light of the new science. No strikingly new doctrine of man emerged but, as the empirical spirit gained control, the classic doctrines were re-evaluated. There was no promise yet of an independent science of psychology; but the other sciences—astronomy, physics and the medical sciences—were freeing themselves from traditional philosophy, and many of their empirical findings were to become later part of the subject matter of a scientific psychology.

LEONARDO THE PIONEER

Perhaps no Renaissance figure typifies the new spirit of inquiry better than does Leonardo da Vinci (1452–1519). He is generally known as one of the greatest painters of all time, creator of such famous pictures as the *Mona Lisa* and *The Last Supper*. Even if all his paintings had been lost, however, he would still deserve an important place in the history of science; for through his art he opened up new problems for the scientist. The student of Leonardo's pictures always marvels at his mastery of light and shade, color and perspective. The pictures are not only beautiful; they also look "real." Objects are depicted "as they are seen," *i.e.,* in their true colors and proportions, in their proper distance perspective, with lights and shadows playing on them as they do in real life. Leonardo realized that to represent nature correctly one had to study nature. This led him to anatomy, the geometry of visual perspective, the physics of illumination. The facts he needed were not in the commentaries on Aristotle, so he sought them out for himself. He performed experiments, developed theories, and applied his theories not only in his art but also to solve various problems of civil and military engineering. His notebooks are still valuable sources of scientific fact and insight.

Leonardo is important in the history of science not only for his discoveries, many of which are basic to the psychology of perception, but also, and perhaps even more significantly, for his exemplification of the empirical approach. When confronted with a problem he thought about it, of course, and he consulted the records of the past; but then, taking nothing on faith but the assurance that meticulous observation will yield truth, he insisted on looking at the facts himself and drawing his own conclusions.

This faith that empirical inquiry will yield truth was the outstanding characteristic of the new scientific movement. Most of the early modern scientists were devoutly religious, some Roman Catholic, some Protestant; and many found themselves in trouble with the church. In challenging the authority of tradition they were not in their opinion denying their religion; they were discovering, they believed, new and hitherto unknown ways in which the greatness of God is made manifest. The new science was, it is true, a threat to established religion; but the real conflict between religion and science was yet to come.

THE COPERNICAN REVOLUTION

Since the beginning of the Christian era the accepted cosmology was geocentric, *i.e.,* the theory that the earth is the stationary center of the universe about which the planets revolve in concentric circular paths. Although Aristotle had expounded such a theory, it is usually referred to as the Ptolemaic system, after the second century Graeco-Egyptian astronomer Ptolemy. Ptolemy's collation and systematization of the work of the Alexandrian astronomers, known as the *Almagest,* was preserved in Arabic scholarship and during the Middle Ages was accepted by the Christian Church as the authoritative work on astronomy. The Ptolemaic system was for obvious reasons congenial to the Christian theologians. It was easy to teach, since it readily explained the observed movements of the sun and stars; it gave man a central place in the universe, without which the Christian doctrine of salvation would be difficult to defend; and, above all, it was in agreement with the Biblical account of the Creation. In mediaeval Christian teaching Ptolemy ranked with Aristotle and Galen as one who might not be challenged.

The revolt against the Ptolemaic system was initiated by Niklas Koppernigk (1473–1543), a Polish astronomer who Latinized his name as Copernicus. What has come to be known as the Copernican system is a heliocentric astronomy, *i.e.,* the theory that the sun is the center of the universe about which the various planets, including the earth, revolve. Copernicus was a devout Roman Catholic priest, with a passion for the observation of the stars. His observations, which he recorded over a period of many years, forced him to the conclusion that Ptolemy was wrong—that the earth revolves about the sun, not the sun about the earth. He wrote his conclusions in a book, *De revolutionibus orbium coelestium,* which, possibly because he feared the implications of his theory for Christian faith, possibly because he was simply frightened, was not published until after his death. His friends, who edited it for publication, were careful to present it as "hypothesis" rather than as fact, with the result that the book was not at once banned but was merely "corrected" by the official censor. The book was widely read; and it started a scientific revolution.

The three great figures in the Copernican revolution are: the Scandinavian Tycho Brahe (1546–1601), the Florentine Galileo

(1564–1642), and the German Kepler (1571–1630). Copernicus, in spite of his passion for accurate observation, had never questioned the Greek belief that astral movement must be circular, since the circle is the perfect form. In fact, he was not even advancing a new theory, for in the third century B.C. Aristarchus had developed a heliocentric astronomy. What is significant is that after centuries of blind acceptance of authority a man with clear eyes and a clear head took a fresh look at the phenomena and drew independent conclusions. Tycho Brahe extended and corrected the observations. Building on Brahe's findings Kepler loosened the grip of tradition still more, demonstrating that the path of a planet is elliptical rather than circular, that its velocity varies inversely as its distance from the sun, and that the different motions of all the planets can be encompassed by a single mathematical statement. Galileo, a contemporary of Kepler's and a friend through correspondence, shocked the orthodox world still further. The telescope had just been invented. Galileo built one for himself, searched the skies and discovered the satellites of Jupiter. Almost as cherished as the doctrine of geocentrism was the belief that there were only seven heavenly bodies. Here was a demonstration that there are more, possibly many more, than seven, that refined observation can yield facts not to be found in the inspired writings of the past. Even more important, although less disturbing at the time, were Galileo's studies of the dynamics of projectiles, of falling bodies and of pendular motion. With the crude measuring instruments of his day, many of which he himself invented or improved, he was able to demonstrate that the motions of all bodies under all conditions are governed by a single set of laws. The grand synthesis of Newton was yet to come, but in the work of Galileo we have an expression of the faith that the physical world, which includes the stars, in one system, is to be understood in terms of the same laws.

The Copernican theory met with resistance everywhere, for it threatened to undermine Christian doctrine. Copernicus himself, we have noted, refused to publish during his lifetime. Tycho Brahe refrained from any daring generalizations. Kepler, as a Protestant, was safe from the Inquisition, although the Copernican theory was roundly condemned by both Luther and Calvin. Protestantism had not yet developed a policing agency, but it could not condone a theory that was so flagrantly in contradiction to Biblical teaching. It was Galileo who bore the brunt of the persecution. An opponent of Aristotle from the early days of his scientific career, he welcomed the Copernican interpretation, shared his thoughts and his discoveries with the Protestant Kepler, and incautiously wrote a book which, while ostensibly presenting the Copernican theory as "hypothesis," actually demolished all the arguments against it. This was sufficient for his enemies. At the age of seventy, crippled by rheumatism and almost blind, he was summoned before the Inquisition. There is no evidence that he was actually tortured, although the Inquisition always meant the threat of torture. Under the stress of the examination, however, Galileo abjectly recanted a doctrine that was later to be accepted by all scientists and by the church that had condemned it. He lived for several more years, and the story is that he continued to have guilt feelings, not because he had accepted a doctrine that was judged to be false, but because in his fear of death at the stake he had denied something he believed to be true.

The implications of the Copernican revolution are so profound that they stagger the imagination. For the scientist, of course, it meant a tremendous liberation, the opening up of exciting new worlds to explore; and after Copernicus the tempo of scientific activity mounted rapidly. For the representatives of orthodox religion it was so frightening as to render impossible any rational consideration of it. For the average man it was simply bewildering. For centuries people had believed that man was the center of the universe, created in the image of God, the special object of God's love and God's wrath. Now it was being suggested that man is an insignificant creature, living briefly on one of several planets in a universe of unknown size. The Copernican theory did not detract from the greatness of God, but it certainly threatened the basis of man's self-esteem.

THE NEWTONIAN REVOLUTION

In the thinking of Galileo we have the beginnings of a unified theory of the physical universe. It is one of the quirks of history that the year of Galileo's death saw the birth of the man who was to achieve the promised integration. Sir Isaac Newton (1642–1727),

English mathematician and physicist, professor at Cambridge University, leader in the newly founded Royal Society, was just one of many scientists in Western Europe who were eagerly cultivating the fields that Copernicans had reclaimed. Any one of his special contributions, *e.g.*, the calculus (shared with Leibnitz), his formulation of the laws of motion (anticipated in part by Galileo) and his demonstration that white light is a compound of colored lights, would have gained him a place in the history of science. It was his genius for synthesis, however, his vision of the whole physical universe as intelligible in terms of a single set of laws, that justifies us in speaking of the Newtonian Revolution and the Newtonian Era.

The Newtonian synthesis is seen most clearly in his generalization of the law of gravitation. In Kepler's observations of planetary motion and Galileo's measurements of the acceleration of falling bodies he found facts which could be encompassed by a single principle. All bodies, whether they be stars or bullets or oceans, attract one another in such a way as to affect each other's motion, the amount of attraction being directly proportional to the product of their masses and inversely proportional to the square of the distance between them. Here is a principle which points towards the ultimate unification of all the sciences of physical nature.

Newton's achievement was so great, and his success so amply rewarded, that, as Bertrand Russell wryly remarked, he was in danger of becoming another Aristotle. The Newtonian system triumphed in the seventeenth century, dominated the sciences of the eighteenth and nineteenth centuries, set the pattern for the modern doctrine of man, and in the mid-twentieth century is still present in our implicit assumptions. The "new science" of Copernicus, Kepler and Galileo was contending against Aristotle. It may be that the "new science" of today will have to vanquish Newton before it is fully liberated.

Newton was not an irreligious man. He believed in God; but he pushed God farther and farther out of the universe. His faith was that, as more and more facts are observed, recorded and analyzed, natural laws will be revealed that will completely explain the facts. If there is a purpose behind the universe, it is a purpose that operates "in accordance with the rules of the game." The scientist discovers the rules, not by communing with God, but by looking at the facts.

The elementary facts of nature are: (1) absolute space, consisting of points; (2) absolute time, consisting of moments; (3) particles of matter, existing in space, enduring through time, and possessing mass; and (4) forces, which operate in space and time to produce changes of motion in matter. All of these are measurable. To explain a natural event is accordingly to restate it mathematically in these terms. Now that metric devices have been standardized this is frequently referred to as the Centimeter-Gram-Second, or CGS, system (C for space, G for mass, S for time; with force considered as reducible to the other three). If we recall Aristotle's doctrine of causality we note at once that Newton's system of explanation rests primarily on Aristotle's material and efficient causes, *i.e.,* force operating on matter in space and time. Formal causes might also be included if we consider form to be merely a spatio-temporal configuration of matter; although this was not Aristotle's conception of it. But there is no place for final causes. One may not, as a Newtonian scientist, invoke teleological explanations.

Newton's system clearly foreshadows a revival of materialism. The basic concepts are those of Democritus, and the ideal of an objective science of nature is the same. But Newton had in addition a bulging storehouse of empirical fact and a set of mathematical tools that the Greeks had never discovered. For the first time in history materialism was able to defend itself with weapons of its own choosing. It would be incorrect, however, to say that the seventeenth century saw an immediate swing to a materialistic doctrine of man. Newton himself avoided the question of man's place in nature, and most of his contemporaries tried manfully to reconcile their science and their religion. Indeed, it was not until the mid-eighteenth century, *e.g.,* La Mettrie's *L'homme machine* (1748), that a frankly materialistic psychology was systematically expounded. Nevertheless the movement was underway. After Newton it was inevitable that the beautiful simplicity of physical science should set the pattern for psychological analysis.

THE REVOLUTION IN THE LIFE SCIENCES

The revolution in the medical and biological sciences was slower and less dramatic than it was in astronomy and physics. Nevertheless we note that during a scant two centuries there was a radical reorientation in the approach to the biology of organisms. It is true that Darwin's great challenge was not to come until mid-nineteenth century, but in some fields, notably in anatomy and physiology, the groundwork of a genuine science had been laid by the year 1700. The hero of the revolution, if one name is to be selected, was William Harvey (1578–1657) who in 1628 published his treatise on the circulation of the blood. Harvey's discovery did not lead to a Newtonian type of synthesis, but it broke down one more barrier to a scientific understanding of organisms, and it released a wave of productive research.

The students of life processes, like the students of physical nature, also had to contend with Authority. The authorities were: Aristotle, Galen and the Bible. Aristotle had classified plants and animals according to principles that remained essentially unchallenged for nearly two thousand years, and had worked out a crude physiology. Hippocrates (ca. 460–370 B.C.), the highminded "father" of the medical profession, had much earlier developed what was virtually a handbook of medical practice, including interesting speculations about the nature of health and disease, about the proper treatment of different kinds of disorder, and about the specific functions of different organs of the body; and most of the other Greek philosophers had had their say about the theory of organismic functioning. It was Galen (ca. 129–199), however, who systematized the medical lore of the Greeks and was to become the approved medical authority of orthodox Christianity. The result was that for fourteen centuries the progress of the medical sciences was arrested. It is true that during this period Arabic and Jewish physicians were active and creative; but it was against the Galenic system that the new biological science of the Renaissance had to battle.

Galen's theories are not to be disparaged; they represent the best that the second century could provide. What is to be deplored is that they were elevated almost to the position of sacred dogma. The details of Galen's system need not concern us here. His gross anatomy of the body was fairly good; including a differentiation between sensory and motor nerves; in his physiology he carried the doctrine of functional localization far beyond Hippocrates; he also developed further the Hippocratic theory that the differences in human temperament are due to varying combinations of fundamental "humors" (a foretaste of modern endocrinology), thereby suggesting a natural basis for the theory of character; and he catalogued the specific treatments that are appropriate to specific ailments. Galen's system might at first glance be considered a materialistic doctrine of man, since he made every effort to relate psychological phenomena to underlying bodily processes; but there was also the doctrine of the *pneuma*. It was the *pneuma* that gained him his position in Christian orthodoxy.

Pneuma, like *psuche,* originally meant breath or air. *Pneuma* was later translated as "spirit," *psuche* as "soul". *Pneuma,* in Aristotle, was the "fiery spirit" that distinguishes living from nonliving things, a partial manifestation of *psuche.* In later history the terms "vital spirit" and "animal spirit" were to be used. The Greeks were baffled by the problem of explaining the difference between the living and the nonliving, and were content to postulate a *pneuma.* Galen's inclusion of the pneumatic principle legitimized him as a non-materialist. The machinery of the body might be represented in materialistic terms, but its functioning required a spiritualistic explanation. A nonmaterial *pneuma* must be invoked if we are to explain why organisms do what they do; and this nonmaterial principle could be revealed only by the theologians.

At the beginning of the sixteenth century the practice of medicine was in a sad state. Like Law and Theology, Medicine was taught dogmatically as a body of doctrine that might not be challenged. The ancient authorities, particularly Galen, had established the facts and laid down the rules. The future physician had simply to master the doctrine and learn Galen's rules. The doctrine was a strange combination of metaphysics, theology and science. The practice of medicine was an even stranger combination of magic and common sense. Some herbs were known to be "good for" certain ailments, although the explanation of their efficacy might be completely wrong. The letting of blood, a popular remedy for almost any disease, was frequently helpful; and the negative cases could be referred to God's unknown purposes. The mediaeval physician could even, on the basis of astrology, diagnose an illness, without having seen the patient, and prescribe the proper remedy. If the remedy did not work, he could always invoke a supernatural explanation.

A modern anthropologist, looking at mediaeval medicine, would rank it with the sorcery and magic of the primitive cultures he was studying. It is no wonder that Galileo, whose father was pushing him in the direction of medicine, decided that it was a dull and unpromising field, far less exciting than physics and astronomy. At the beginning of the Renaissance the medical sciences offered little challenge to the inquiring mind.

During the sixteenth century the grip of Galen on the medical sciences began to weaken. Although the dissection of human bodies was still officially disapproved by the Church it was unostentatiously practiced, and the number of demonstrable errors in Galen's system of anatomy mounted. An important role in the new anatomical studies was played by the artists. Both Leonardo (1452–1515) and Michelangelo (1475–1564) conducted extensive dissections and made significant discoveries; and many of the lesser artists became interested in the sketching of anatomical parts. By 1543 it was possible for Andreas Vesalius (1514–1564) to publish a beautifully illustrated volume that was to establish him as the founder of modern anatomy. The victory over Galen was not immediate, of course, for the traditionalists were still unwilling to accept the evidence of their eyes when this conflicted with the writings of Authority. Nevertheless Vesalius had delivered a powerful blow.

The final blow was delivered by Harvey when he disposed of the doctrine of the *pneuma*. Galen had taught that the spirits are generated in the heart and puffed out through the body by way of the arteries. In both the arteries and the veins there is a constant ebb and flow, like the tides, arterial blood being diluted by spirits. Vesalius had corrected Galen's anatomy of the heart without being able to explain its functioning. In 1628, Harvey's book, "On the motion of the heart and the blood," demonstrated for the first time that there is a single system that operates in circular fashion by way of a set of valves, the same blood being pumped out through the arteries and returned through the veins. There was no place in Harvey's physiology of circulation for a special pneumatic principle; the whole process could be explained in natural-scientific, possibly in mechanical, terms.

The doctrine of the *pneuma* died hard. Harvey's findings were not welcomed and, even when his theory of circulation was conceded to be right, the spirits continued to live in the nerves and the brain. The flow of blood might be accepted as a natural process; but, before the days of electricity, what but an immaterial substance could flow through the nerves? Physiology had to wait for more than two hundred years before it could begin to grapple successfully with the nervous system, and we are still barely beyond a beginning. Nevertheless, Harvey's discovery held out the promise that one day all the processes of the body might be subsumed under the laws of nature.

The three revolutions we have been discussing belong together as part of a single movement. The New Science that was born in the sixteenth century was only a partial expression of a new *Weltanschauung* that was developing, a new World View that reveals itself in the art, literature, religion, politics, economics and social organization of the period. Our present interest must be limited to its implications for: (1) the meaning of science, and (2) the doctrine of man.

THE MEANING OF THE NEW SCIENCE

The New Science was essentially a revolt against Aristotle—not so much the Aristotle of the fifth century B.C. as the reinterpreted Aristotle of the Middle Ages. The real Aristotle might well have been welcomed by the Moderns as a kindred spirit; but, by the beginning of the sixteenth century, he had come to represent all that was blindly traditional, the great Authority who had to be unseated. When we speak of Aristotelianism we refer to a mediaeval world view that had had its origins in Aristotle but that had become heavily loaded with Christian theology.

It has become customary to think of Sir Francis Bacon (1561–1626) as the spokesman for the new science in its revolt against Aristotle. Bacon was an English patrician whose life was entangled in politics, but whose passion was the new science. As a scientist he was never more than a dilettante, but as a writer he was extremely effective. His brilliant style (which has tempted some to identify him as the author of Shakespeare's plays) and his grasp of the essentials of the new movement have ensured his place in the history of science. His *Novum Organum* (1620), named after Aristotle's *Organon,* boldly proposed that in science the Aristotelian method of "deduction" be replaced by the method of "induction". He was wrong in his interpretation of Aristotle; as we have seen, Aristotle's logic was deductive, but much of his science was inductive.

Bacon was right, however, in his charge against the mediaeval Aristotelians, who scorned the facts of observation. Bacon may have been overoptimistic about the inductive method, but he brilliantly stated the faith of the new science—the faith that through observation truth can be established.

If Bacon was the best spokesman for the new science, Galileo Galilei (1564–1642) was certainly its greatest personification. He was a rebel from the beginning, not against the social order but against what he believed to be false doctrine, and he died with the hope that his rebellion would grow into a revolution; which it did. He is in many ways the dramatist's conception of the scientist, as Socrates is of the philosopher. (Indeed, plays and novels have been written about both men). Kindly, unpractical and gullible in his personal affairs, he was fiercely intolerant of stupidity in any form, single-minded when he was on the trail of a new fact, passionate in his insistence on accuracy of observation, but still wide-eyed with wonder and excitement as he contemplated the unknown. We have the picture of a boundless curiosity, controlled but not inhibited by rigorous intellectual discipline. Galileo was a moderately devout Christian, but for him the cardinal sin was not disloyalty to the Church but disloyalty to the facts of observation.

Galileo's specific contributions were all in the physical sciences. We have already noted the importance of his discoveries for the later Newtonian synthesis; and a full account would include many more. What concerns us here, however, is the approach which he represents. The Galilean mode of thought, as contrasted with the Aristotelian, was to set the pattern for the science of the future. The salient features of this new mode of thought may be summarized briefly.

(1) The *problems* of the new science were still the classic problems of philosophy, but with the emphasis on the problem of explaining the nature of the physical world. Science was struggling to emancipate itself from theology, but the scientist still thought of himself as a philosopher. Even today there are some university chairs of physics that bear the title Natural Philosophy. The scientist of the Renaissance hoped to be able to explain the physical world without benefit of theology; he was beginning to have the same hope in connection with the structure and functioning of organisms; but he was still far from thinking that the essential nature of man would yield itself to a natural explanation. The possibility of a science of man was nothing but a dim glimmer.

(2) The *data* of the new science were no longer the dicta of the Authorities but the facts of observation. What you see or hear or touch is a fact—to be checked, of course, because the senses are fallible—but to be believed when it stands up under scrutiny, even if it conflicts with Authority. The telescope and the microscope were providing new data. The traditionalists rejected them because they were incompatible with established doctrine. The new science eagerly accepted such data, and proceeded to make the theory conform to the facts. Today we like to think we are factually minded. It is difficult for us to understand the person who rejects a fact of observation because it does not fit his theory, although every one of us is guilty, albeit unconsciously, of ignoring disagreeable facts. In the Middle Ages a fact of observation, like the satellites of Jupiter, could be flatly rejected, not because the observation was incorrect but because the acceptance of its consequences would be too disrupting.

(3) In the realm of *methodology* the trend of the new science was even more radical. Part of this trend is represented by the shift of emphasis from the deductive to the inductive method. As we have noted, however, this distinction is not wholly satisfactory. Deduction is the inferential process whereby particular conclusions are drawn from general propositions assumed to be true, the classical example being Aristotelian syllogism. Induction, on the other hand, is supposed to be the process whereby general propositions are logically derived from the examination of a great number of particular instances, as in the generalization that newborn babies have a powerful grasping reflex. Deduction leads to certainty, if we assume that the premises are correct: induction usually leads to a statement of probability, since we can seldom be sure that we have examined all the particular instances. Thus, if we assume that all men are mortal we may deduce with certainty that John Smith, a man, is mortal. If, however, we try inductively to establish the proposition that all men are mortal, all we can do is count the cases, thereby rendering the proposition more and more probable; but there is always the possibility that someday we may encounter an immortal man.

It is true that the scholars of the Middle Ages preferred the deductive method, and that the new scientists of the Renaissance were inductive in the sense that they tried to generalize from the facts of observation. Copernicus was being inductive when he faithfully recorded the positions of the planets before he drew his conclusions, and so was Galileo when he observed the relation between the length of a pendulum and the period of its swing. What is important, however, is that in each of these cases, and in every other development of the new science, the scientist was not passively inspecting the facts; he was testing an hypothesis. Newton did not spend his life measuring the rate of fall of all possible apples from all possible trees. He made as many observations as were necessary to permit an hypothesis, deduced the consequences of the hypothesis, and then sought for the crucial observation that might provide the test. The new scientists were not challenging the deductive method as such; rather, they were challenging the assumptions from which earlier deductions had been made.

The really significant methodological contribution of the new science was its refinement of the methods of deriving and testing hypotheses. The best example is to be found in the notion of the crucial experiment. An experiment, in everyday language, is a question put to nature in such a way that nature can provide a clear and unequivocal answer. Any good experiment requires (a) an initial hypothesis, (b) a set of predictions, derived logically from the hypothesis, that under such-and-such conditions such-and-such will happen, and (c) controlled conditions of observations which permit the observer to determine with a high degree of probability whether or not his predictions were correct. In a crucial experiment the hypothesis is either confirmed or negated. More commonly, the hypothesis is strengthened or weakened, and further experiments are necessary. Galileo, in his experiments on falling bodies, began with the Aristotelian dictum that the heavier the body the faster it will fall. Aristotle had deduced this from his principle of inherent properties, but had never tested it experimentally. Galileo set up the alternative hypothesis that speed of fall has nothing to do with weight, contrived an experiment (possibly from the leaning tower of Pisa) in which bodies of the same size but different weights were dropped simultaneously from the same height and definitely disproved Aristotle. This in itself was a negative finding. Since he had carefully timed the fall at different distances from the starting point, however, he discovered new facts that led to a new hypothesis about the acceleration of falling bodies. Newton was to incorporate this positive finding into his generalized law of gravitation.

The experimental method is best exemplified by the physical

sciences, in which the scientist can control his variables. As we have seen, however, it was rapidly assimilated by the life sciences. Astronomy has sometimes been considered a nonexperimental science, since the astronomer cannot control the things he is observing. The astronomer can, however, formulate hypotheses, make predictions, and test these under controlled conditions of observation; and these are the proper criteria of an experiment. But the science of human nature was yet to be born. The Renaissance gave birth to a new scientific method, but even the best of the Renaissance scientists did not dare to apply it to man.

(4) It was in its *explanatory constructs* that the new science departed most drastically from tradition. To explain is to make clear; and the scientist strove for clarity. For centuries the Church had been impressing on man the limitations of his own wisdom. The mind of God is unfathomable. God works in a mysterious way his wonders to perform. Man must be content with partial understanding; the rest he must simply believe. For a Galileo or a Newton such a restriction on human curiosity was unacceptable. The scientist was willing to concede that some things may be ultimately unintelligible except on the basis of faith; but, as he stubbornly continued to observe, measure and experiment, he discovered that more and more of the puzzles of nature were becoming clear. He was actually explaining in natural terms phenomena that had hitherto been unintelligible. Small wonder, then, that the new science began to generate a faith that ultimately science would displace theology. There is little evidence that in the sixteenth and seventeenth centuries such a faith was more than a dim hope. Nevertheless the seeds had been sown; scientists were uncovering more and more of the secrets of nature; and more and more explanations were now being given "without benefit of clergy."

What did the new science consider a proper explanation? Here are a few principles that seem to have been basic.

(a) The world that we live in is a world of matter. It may have been created originally by God, and faith in God may be compatible with faith in science; but God may not be invoked as an explanation of any particular thing or event in the material world. As we have noted, the new scientists were not irreligious; they merely resented the intrusion of theology into science.

(b) The material world is governed by natural law; and natural law is inflexible, permitting of no exceptions. The statement that the exception proves the rule (*Exceptio regulam probat*) has often been confusedly interpreted to mean that somehow or other the presence of an exception implies the existence of a law. Correctly translated it means simply that the exception is a test of the law; if there is even one exception, then we have not stated the true law and we must consequently search for a better formulation. (In a Galilean experiment on the rate of fall of bodies we note that a feather may fall more slowly than does a stone. We might consider the feather as an exception to the law. It ceases to be an exception, however, when we recognize the fact of friction with the air. Objects fall through a medium, and the resistance of the medium must be included in the statement of the law.)

(c) Natural law has no place for purposes, transcendent or immanent; purposes are interpretations, not facts. The new science was opposed to teleology. Aristotle's final causes and, less clearly, his formal causes were considered unnecessary.

(d) Causation is a necessary connection between a thing, condition or event and the antecedent or concomitant things, conditions or events. Causation is thus a one-way process. That which has not yet happened cannot cause that which is now happening. The new science gave a special meaning to the concept of causation that was to dominate thinking for three centuries.

(e) Explanatory constructs must be as simple and modest as possible. William of Occam, a reported fourteenth century Franciscan, is reported to have said that *Entia non sunt multiplicanda praeter necessitatem,* meaning that we should always try to explain in the simplest possible terms. This became known as "Occam's razor," and the new scientists took the law seriously. It was Newton who gave the new science its simplest constructs: space, time, matter, force. These were the terms in which the whole material universe would eventually be explained. Where nature seemed to resist explanation there was still the faith that eventually nature's resistance might be broken down.

(f) The laws of nature are absolute, but our understanding of them is imperfect. The truth exists, but the best we can say is an approximation of the truth. The new scientists realized that their best judgments were statements of probability. To accept the principle of probability is to concede that the whole of the truth can never be known at one time. The mathematical theory of probability was not to be formulated until much later, but the new scientists accepted the principle. New facts add to understanding; the understanding mind looks for further facts; and further facts enrich understanding, and raise new questions; the process is never complete. This was the spirit of the new science.

(g) The behavior of objects and events in nature cannot be explained in terms of properties and tendencies presumed to be inherent in them. Thus Aristotle was incorrect in asserting that bodies fall because of an inherent property of heaviness. A stick of wood may fall through the air but rise if released under water. To understand its motion we must know something about its relation to the medium through which it moves. Weight, as Galileo and Newton demonstrated, is a relative concept. So are heat, velocity and a host of other standard concepts of physics. In rejecting the doctrine of inherent properties the new scientists were not proposing a Protagorean type of relativism; in fact, the Newtonian system rests on the assumption of absolute space and time. We may insist that our explanatory constructs be relational, and at the same time believe that these relations are embedded in natural law. The generalized law of gravitation, for instance, affirmed a set of relationships as true for all bodies under all circumstances. The falling of a body may not be due to an inherent tendency to fall, but the laws that govern the interaction of bodies in a gravitational field are inherent in nature.

The concept of "field" is important. Although the term did not become popular until after Faraday's nineteenth century work on electricity and magnetism, it was implicit in the thinking of the new scientists of the Renaissance. In challenging the doctrine of inherent properties the new scientists were asserting that the laws of nature are not laws of individual things and events but laws of interaction; that the individual is unintelligible except in the context of its "field." "Field theory," in physics, in biology and in psychology, was later to become a movement of major significance.

(h) Mere classification does not explain. Aristotle's science was a magnificient achievement in classification, and no scientist since Aristotle has seriously questioned the value of an orderly presentation of the facts of his field in categories, subcategories and sub-subcategories. It simplifies our thinking if we can identify as mammals all warm-blooded vertebrates that nourish their young by means of milk-secreting organs, as primates those mammals that have reached a high order of development, and as humans those primates that have developed a capacity for abstract reasoning. We can observe and generalize what, as a class, worms and spiders and monkeys and human babies do. Having made the generalization, we can predict with some accuracy how this particular insect or baby will behave under specified conditions of stimulation. But are we explaining the dog's chasing of the cat when we say that chasing cats is a characteristic of "dogginess?" or that the moth's approach to the lamp is due to the fact that all moths have a phototropic tendency? The new scientists were not satisfied with such explanations.

The danger in the classificatory approach lies in the temptation to accept one principle of classification as final. If fish are creatures that swim about in water, then whales are fish; if mammals are creatures that nourish their young by milk-secreting glands, then whales are mammals. Is the whale a fish or a mammal? From the point of view of tradition this is an important question, for fish and mammals were supposed to be different classes.

THE NEW SCIENCE AND THE DOCTRINE OF MAN

The new science, we have noted, did not give us immediately a new doctrine of man. Man in the sixteenth century certainly had no more, and perhaps considerably less, self knowledge than he had had in the time of Socrates. He was muddled by his theology, confused about his place in the new universe that was opening up, and insecure as to his place in society. Yet out of bewilderment comes curiosity. It was inevitable that Renaissance man, as he succeeded in unlocking more and more of the secrets of the physical universe, should raise anew all the old questions about his own place in the total scheme. The Renaissance was a rebirth of philosophy as it was of science, and in the new philosophy the psychological problem came more and more clearly into focus.

The essential challenge of the new science to the doctrine of man can be stated very simply: Can man be regarded as a part of the natural world, conforming to natural law, to be understood in terms of the principles of natural science? Or must man be accorded a special place in the universe and a special set of laws? The first alternative seemed to be supported by the new heliocentric astronomy, by the imposing developments in physics and by the dramatic discoveries about the machinery of organismic functioning. The new science held out the promise that the simple laws of space, time, matter and force might eventually encompass all of human behavior. On the other hand were the dictates of the Church and the evidence of direct experience. Can we lightly cast aside the accumulated wisdom of centuries? Can we deny the unique facts of consciousness, our feelings of freedom and responsibility and doubt? These alternatives were to dominate psychological thinking for centuries to come.

The doctrine of man implicit in the new science was a materialistic doctrine. Religion struggled against it, but it was a losing battle. Step by step the scientists were extending the realm of natural law. Religion made one strategic withdrawal after another, capitulating first to the Copernican astronomy, then to a mechanistic physiology, and finally to the Darwinian theory of evolution. Science had begun its forward march.

4

The Persistent Problems

Redefined by the Philosophers

THE EARLY HISTORY of modern psychology is to be found in the history of modern philosophy. The new science may have presented the challenge, but it was the philosophers who undertook the task of re-examining the doctrine of man. We must remember, of course, that the line between science and philosophy was still a dim one, as were the lines dividing the different branches of science. A man like Descartes is usually listed as a philosopher, but he is also granted a chapter in the history of mathematics, of physiology and, as we shall see, of psychology. Newton, whom we all think of as a scientist, speculated unashamedly about problems that would now be considered philosophical. When we speak of philosophy in the seventeenth and eighteenth centuries we are thus referring, not to a professional class of persons, but to types of problems and types of interest. The problems of psychology were in this sense accepted as philosophical problems.

The psychological problems that preoccupied the early modern philosophers were the same as those that had fascinated the ancient Greeks—the relation between mind and body, the basis of knowledge, the basis of individual conduct, the nature of the good society—but this time they were viewed in the context of a different kind of world. There were new facts and new perspectives; the pat answers of tradition were no longer self-evident; the ancients had been proved wrong in so many ways that it might be that their theories of human nature were also wrong. We need not be unduly upset if we find the moderns merely restating what had been said long before. The

111

translation of an old problem into a new language sometimes enables us to see it in a new way and lures us on to further inquiry. This is what happened in the seventeenth and eighteenth centuries. The philosophers, living in a new kind of society, challenged by facts that the Greeks had scarcely dreamed of, were compelled to rethink their doctrine of man. The result was an upsurge of psychological interest such as had not been seen since the days of Aristotle.

Our interest here is less in the thinkers than in their thoughts. Nevertheless, we must have some understanding of the individuals who played such an important role in the modern reformulation of the problems of psychology. They stand out in startling contrast to mediaeval figures like Thomas Aquinas and Abelard, and even to the Greeks. The Greeks who figure in our story were for the most part professional scholars; the Mediaevals were professional churchmen; the Early Moderns could be anything. Some were Roman Catholics, some Protestants; most of them were laymen, rather than clericals; many were university professors; a few had independent fortunes, but many others had nonacademic positions, eking out their livelihood by their writing, and at least one, Spinoza, supported himself by constructing optical equipment. The psychology of the early modern period reflects the attempt of men in many walks of life to meet the challenge not only of the new science but of a society that needed a new foundation.

Let us take a quick glance at the political and social background of the seventeenth and eighteenth centuries, and then at a few of the outstanding philosophers who dominated the period.

THE POLITICAL AND SOCIAL BACKGROUND

(1) The hub of the world was now in Northern Europe. When we try to visualize the power structure of the world at any given time we inevitably see one or more geographic points from which radiate lines of influence. In mid-twentieth century those nodal points might be New York (or Washington) and Moscow. When we think of the fifth century B.C. we think of Athens. A few hundred years later the hub was in Rome; and for many centuries Rome, the seat of Roman Catholicism, continued to be the center of the civilized world. By the

beginning of the sixteenth century other centers of power had come into being, Florence, Bologna and Venice, for instance, but also Paris and London. By the end of the eighteenth century the Italian states had become peripheral. The hub of the world, depending on your point of view, was in Paris or in London. London was the center of commerce and industry, Paris the center of the Arts. London was the heart of a great mercantile empire, Paris the rendezvous of writers, painters, musicians and scientists. France and Great Britain (after the union with Scotland in 1707 England ceased to be a political entity) were bitter rivals in every field; the occasional periods of peace were merely interludes between wars. Nevertheless, the two cultures were complementary. Together they generated the ideas that were to dominate the subsequent development of western civilization. By the end of the eighteenth century all roads were leading to London or Paris.

(2) By the beginning of the seventeenth century the new world across the seas was no longer merely a great unknown that invited exploration; it was a new world that could be settled, developed and exploited. The Spaniards had taken the lead in colonization. With ruthless efficiency they had conquered most of what is now Latin America, established strongholds, enslaved the natives, and filled their coffers with the new found wealth. With similar efficiency they propagated the Christian faith. The French and English had been active in exploration but not in colonization. For them it was simpler to profit from Spanish enterprise by plundering Spanish treasure ships.

Spain's position in Europe was, however, rapidly weakening. The crushing defeat of her Invincible Armada in 1588 left England and France in command of the seas, and the successful revolt against Spain in the Low Countries marked the emergence of a vigorous Dutch navy. Naval power had become the index of strength, and was to remain the index of strength for three hundred years. The seventeenth century witnessed a furious competitive race among the naval powers for overseas colonies. The Dutch were formidable competitors in the west, settling and holding for many years the region of New York and the upper Hudson valley, but their greatest exploits were in South Africa and the Southwest Pacific. The real rivals in the New World were France and England, France in Canada and the West Indies, England in the colonies on the eastern coast. The struggle between England and France was simply extended to the New World. In 1763 the British finally obtained France's surrender of Canada, only to be forced a few years later to yield independence to her own thirteen colonies on the Atlantic seaboard

(3) At the beginning of the seventeenth century the standard form of government in Europe was the monarchy. England was still ruled by the Tudors, France by the Bourbons, Spain by the Hapsburgs. The king (or queen) was at least nominally the final authority over the life of every subject. Questions were beginning to stir, however. The most common question was: To what extent should the power of the monarch be curbed by the will of the people? A less frequent, and more dangerous, question was: Should any single person have the power to rule except by the authority of the people? There were three types of answer: (a) The "divine right" answer— God had granted the King the right to rule, and there can be no questioning the Will of God; (b) The "parliamentarian" answer—The people need a king, but the king must abide by the rules of the people; and (c) the "republican" answer—We have no need of kings; the people should determine their own destiny.

The British tradition was, and still is, that of a monarchy limited in its power by a freely elected parliament. Since the early thirteenth century the parliament had slowly, and with much fumbling developed a set of traditions and procedures that curbed the freedom of the monarch and guaranteed some measure of social justice to the people. For obvious reasons the relations between king and parliament were not always cordial. During the seventeenth century the struggle flared up into civil war. Charles I defied his parliament, and was defeated in battle, convicted of treason, and executed in 1649. After an eleven year interregnum the monarchy was restored. Charles II attempted to rebuild the power of the throne, but parliament was too stubborn. Later British kings, like George III, had dictatorial impulses, but the victory of parliament in the seventeenth century had established once and for all the principle of limited monarchy.

In France the course of history was different, and the climax more catastrophic. In France the right of the monarch to absolute power had never been seriously questioned. By the seventeenth century the monarchy was so strong that the only insurrections against it, the disturbances of the Fronde (1648–1653), were quelled with little difficulty. We think of the long reign of Louis XIV (1643–1715) as the most picturesque example of absolutism in modern times. The court was the center of the life of France, the king the dictator, whose whim could launch a war or set a new fashion in dress or furniture. Louis XIV patronized the arts and the sciences, but the ostentatious luxury of the court and its callous indifference to the welfare of the common people created a rift that was to lead to a bloody revolution. Less than a century after his death the French people rose in revolt, deposed and executed their king and declared themselves a republic.

The idea of the republic, the state in which the rulers are elected by the people and govern with the people's consent, goes back at least as far as the Greek city-states. During the seventeenth and eighteenth centuries the idea came alive again. When in 1648 the Dutch finally threw off the yoke of Spain they established what they called a republic, although it might equally well be termed a limited monarchy. Cromwell's Commonwealth (1649–1660) was formally a republic, although Cromwell himself ruled as a dictator. It was in the colonies across the Atlantic, however, that the republican idea really began to ferment. The monarch in London might be curbed by his parliament so far as home affairs were concerned, but in the colonies there were no controls. The tough pioneers who were carving out a new life for themselves in the New World resented the domination of a uninformed despot. They declared their independence, won the battle for freedom, and set up the first genuine republic of modern times. The American revolution ended officially in 1783. The French revolution is considered to have begun on July 14, 1789. Since then the monarchies of Europe have gradually disappeared; today they can be counted on the fingers of one hand. The republican idea has expressed itself in many forms, some of which have been indistinguishable from the absolute monarchies of the past, but the march of events is clearly away from the monarchical system.

It is intelligible that during this critical period of history the theory of government should have loomed large in the thoughts of the philosophers. English philosophers like Hobbes, Locke and Adam Smith were deeply concerned about political theory. In France the bold theorizing of Voltaire and Rousseau helped to prepare the way for the revolution. In the colonies the pamphleteering of Thomas Paine (1737–1809) gave expression to the radical new ideas that were developing, and Thomas Jefferson (1743–1826), the "philosopher of American democracy," tried to develop a theoretical base for a workable republic. Everywhere philosophic thought reflected the puzzlement of people about the problems of government.

(4) At the beginning of the seventeenth century one could no longer speak of "the Church"; there were many churches, and the Protestant sects were rapidly multiplying. Roman Catholicism was still firmly entrenched in Italy, Spain, France and Southern Germany, although France had its Protestant minority, the Huguenots, many of whom fled to the American colonies. Protestantism had a stronghold in Geneva, had spread across northern Germany and Holland, and was now securely established in England and Scotland. (Even in Ireland there were some Protestants.) Protestantism was a movement, but not a church. The common protest was always there, the protest against the papacy, but doctrines and practices varied. Luther's Protestantism maintained itself in northern Germany. Calvin's austere version found ready followers in the rugged hills of Scotland, where the Presbyterian tradition took root. The Church of England, established in Elizabeth's days, was in its organization and ritual a compromise with Roman Catholicism.

The struggle between Roman Catholicism and Protestantism was as much a political as it was a religious struggle. England's Henry VIII was not distinguished for his religious devotion, and the fervor with which Protestants and Roman Catholics persecuted each other in seventeenth century England had little of the Christian spirit in it. Each side was fighting for control of the nation, and in this case the Protestants finally won. Within Protestantism, however, there were disagreements that had a genuinely religious basis, although even here there were political overtones. To many Protestants the Established Church of England appeared just as venal as had the Church of Rome at the time of the Reformation. The Puritan movement, which was to play such a large part in American history, was as much a protest within Protestantism as it was a further protest against Roman Catholicism. The Puritan Party that finally unseated Charles I demanded moral as well as political reform. Puritanism was a grim religion, rejecting the aesthetic elements of traditional ritual, emphasizing the virtues of simplicity, self-discipline and hard work, enforcing a rigid code of sexual ethics, and holding out to all sinners the terrifying prospect of eternal damnation.

Puritanism never became as such a religious denomination, but it gave birth to numerous special sects, differing in details of theology or practice but united in their refusal to conform. Presbyterians, Methodists, Baptists, Unitarians, Quakers were all "nonconformists," who were forced out of the established church and were frequently persecuted. It was the nonconformist groups that provided most of the early settlers of the American colonies, and it was in the chill climate of Puritanism that early American history was shaped.

(5) Literature and the arts were entering a period of great creativity. Elizabethan England had produced in Shakespeare (1564–1616) not only literature's greatest master of the English language but also, possibly, its most skillful interpreter of human nature. The subsequent history of literature, on the Continent as well as in England, reveals a growing interest in the nature of human motivation and the basis of human character. Dramatists like Moliere and novelists like Richardson and Fielding were probing to find the reasons why people do what they do, and they were developing techniques whereby human character can be rendered intelligible through *depiction* rather than through formal analysis. The literature of the seventeenth and eighteenth centuries is fully as important for the understanding of modern man as is the science of that period.

A similar statement might be made about the visual arts. The Renaissance painters of Italy had advanced the technique of painting enormously and, in spite of the current insistence on classical themes, artists like Leonardo and Titian had been fascinated by the problem of depicting human emotion. In the Low Countries, however, most of the restrictions were removed. The northern seaport towns, like Bruges, Antwerp, the Hague and Amsterdam, were prosperous and independent. For reasons that still puzzle the historians they produced painters who overshadowed the best that could be found in the court of Louis XIV or in Restoration England. Rubens, Franz Hals, Jordaens, Van Dyck, Rembrandt, Vermeer—to name only the most famous—dealt with subjects of contemporary life, which meant contemporary people. Their technique was magnificent; what interests the psychologist is their preoccupation with the portrayal of real, live human beings. The artists of the Low Countries were looking at people as the scientists of that period were looking at nature.

(7) By the beginning of the seventeenth century the great universities of northern Europe were recognized as the centers of learning. The Italian universities still attracted students, but the flow was to Oxford, Cambridge, Paris and Louvain and to such Dutch and German universities as Leyden, Heidelberg, Cologne and Leipzig. While some of these were still officially under ecclesiastical control, their scholarship was becoming more and more secular. The universities were still preoccupied with the training of future priests, physicians and lawyers, but they were beginning to lodge scholars and scientists whose chief concern was with the advancement of knowledge. The modern European university was to replace the monastery and the church school as the bed in which new ideas were conceived and born.

THE OUTSTANDING PHILOSOPHER-PSYCHOLOGISTS

(1)*Thomas Hobbes* (1588–1679): English political and social philosopher, enthusiastic disciple of the new science, whose long life encompassed and was embroiled in the great struggle between Parliament and the Monarchy. Hobbes was an outspoken materialist, a critic of organized religion, a defender of the idea of absolute monarchy, and an exponent of the psychological theory that man in his natural state is governed by selfish impulse (cf. p. 147). Among his many writings the most important for psychology is his *Humaine Nature* (1650) and his *Leviathan* (1651), in which he develops his psychological and social theories.

(2)*René Descartes* (1596–1650): French mathematician, physiologist and philosopher, during most of his active life a resident of Holland; known to mathematicians particularly for his development of analytic geometry, to physiologists for his mechanistic conception of the functions of the body and for his anticipation of the modern theory of the reflex, to philosophers for his brilliant defense of psychophysical interactionism. Descartes has been so influential in the subsequent history of psychology as to have been characterized by some historians as the "father of modern psychology." The "Cartesian method" is expounded in his delightful essay, *Discourse on Method* (1637), the Cartesian psychology in *The Passions of the Soul* (1650).

(3) *Baruch Spinoza* (1632–1677): Dutch philosopher, reared in the orthodox Jewish tradition but later rejected as a heretic by the Jewish community, so profoundly religious that his religion could be contained by no orthodox theology, the model of the humble philosopher whose sole dedication is to truth. At a different time in another culture Spinoza might have been deified; he is now merely revered. His *Ethics*, published in 1677 after his death, is essentially a religious document, dully scholastic in form but daring in its conclusions. For the history of psychology it is important as the first great attempt of modern times to find a metaphysical system capable of overcoming the dualism of mind and matter and resolving the problem of free will versus determinism. His direct contribution to psychological theory was not great, but his influence was profound.

(4) *John Locke* (1632–1704): English philosopher, economist and political theorist; trained for the medical profession, but engaged during the greater part of his life with political and economic problems. Locke, if not the "father of British empiricism," was at least its first systematic exponent. In his *Essay Concerning Human Understanding* (1690) he took issue with the Cartesian doctrine of innate ideas and laid the groundwork for the empirical theory that has dominated British and American psychology ever since. For him the human mind was a *tabula rasa,* a blank sheet on which anything could be written. In political and economic theory he is regarded as one of the great champions of individual liberty.

(5) *Gottfried Wilhelm von Leibnitz* (1646–1716: German philosopher, mathematician and diplomat, friend of kings and princes in many countries, dilletante in many fields of scholarship. In mathematics Leibnitz is famous as the discoverer (independently of Newton) of the differential calculus. His philosophic system was based on his "monadology, " a difficult and intricate theory based on the assumption of an infinite number of elementary units of force (the monads) which combine in accordance with pre-established law to form the reality we know. Each monad has its psychic aspect, and each monad is independent of all others, the consistency observed in nature being due to a pre-established harmony. Leibnitz accepted the Cartesian doctrine of innate ideas, defending it against Locke's em-

piricism, but rejected Descartes' interactionism in favor of the doctrine of psychophysical parallelism. His principle of pre-established harmony was cruelly satirized in Voltaire's *Candide.* Although the language of the monadology is no longer used, we are still challenged by Leibnitz's argument that mind has a structure of its own and that there are mental processes operating below the level of full consciousness.

(6) *George Berkeley* (1685–1753): Irish ecclesiastic (eventually a bishop), whose frustrated ambition to convert American Indians to Christianity was solaced by his achievements in philosophy. Fascinated by Locke's empirical approach, he applied it in his *Essay Toward a New Theory of Vision* (1709), a work that is still to be reckoned with. In *A Treatise Concerning the Principles of Human Knowledge* (1710) he presented in systematic fashion his doctrine of subjective idealism, which is really a restatement of Plato in the light of the New Science. He is at his wittiest, however, in his *Three Dialogues between Hylas and Philonous* (1713). In the best Socratic style the arguments of Hylas, the believer in primary matter, who is Locke (Gr. *hule*), are neatly demolished by Philonous, the believer in mind (Gr. *nous*).

The philosopher-psychologists of the seventeenth and eighteenth centuries were, as we have seen, drawn from varied backgrounds. Some had medical training, some were active in political life, some were university professors, some pursued philosophy for the sheer love of it. All were challenged by the New Science, all felt themselves hampered by traditional religious doctrine, all were seeking for a doctrine of man that would define his role in a changing and turbulent world. As we try to understand their theories we must never forget that these are the thoughts of men for whom philosophy was not just idle speculation. Heretics were less frequently being burned at the stake, but unorthodox opinions would lead to persecution. To be a philosopher in those days required courage and independence. It is not irrelevant to note that nearly all of the leading philosopher-psychologists whom we are considering were publicly denounced, and several were forced into exile.

The persistent psychological problems that they tried to answer were all posed initially by religion. Can we believe that we have immortal souls when science is steadily demonstrating that the human body is a machine? Can we believe the evidence of our senses as opposed to the evidence of divine revelation, especially when new instruments like the telescope and the microscope are disclosing phenomena which ordinary sense perception cannot apprehend? Can we believe that "the chief end of man is to glorify God and enjoy Him forever" when the scrutiny of man's behavior suggests that he is governed by brute instincts? What can we really believe in? This was the over riding question. The new science had shaken the comfortable theology of the past. The revolutionary movements were demanding a revaluation of man's place in society. The new philosophers rose to meet the challenge. We can understand why for nearly three hundred years the problems of psychology were oriented toward the problems of belief.

THE RELATIONSHIP BETWEEN MIND AND BODY

Our understanding of the mind-body problem is sometimes hampered by linguistic confusions. As long as philosophers were writing in Latin they had at least common words for their concepts, e.g., *anima, spiritus*. When they began to write in the vernacular, however, what seemed to be equivalent words gradually acquired slightly different meanings. In French *anima* became *l'âme* and *spiritus* became *l'esprit*. The parallels in German are *die Seele* and *der Geist*. In both languages the original Latin distinction became blurred, and the two words have sometimes been used interchangeably. In English the meaning was divided three ways. English had the word "soul" (*anima, l'âme, die Seele*) and the word "spirit" (*spiritus, l'esprit, der Geist*), but it also had the word "mind" (derived from the Latin *mens*). The word "mind" gradually absorbed the psychological meaning of "soul" and "spirit," and these two words have, except in their metaphorical and colloquial usage, been returned to theology. Thus we may not assume that when a French author writes about "l'âme primitive" he is thinking of the "soul" in its theological sense; "mind" would be a better translation. Nor may we translate "die geistige Entwicklung des Kindes" as "the spiritual development of the child"; "mental development" would be more appropriate. "Mind" in English became an all-inclusive term to designate "that which is not material".

During the seventeenth and eighteenth centuries virtually every theory of the mind-body relationship was ably presented. The dualistic alternatives are: interactionism and parallelism, defended respectively by Descartes and Leibnitz. The principal monistic alternatives are: idealism and materialism, defended respectively by Berkeley and La Mettrie. A third monistic alternative, sometimes called neutral monism, or the dual-aspect theory, was best expressed by Spinoza. There were no real pluralists, although Spinoza, since he believed that God had an infinite number of attributes, might be classified as a pluralistic monist. No philosopher since then has proposed any significantly different theory.

The problem that confronted the philosophers of the seventeenth century was essentially the same as that which had puzzled the philosophers of the fifth century B.C. Experience forces upon us a distinction between that which is dead, resistant, malleable but ultimately indestructible (matter) and that which is lively, conscious and free (mind, soul, spirit). These seem to be different types of reality, but they also seem to be related to each other in a causal way. How can these two forms of reality be reconciled within a single system? For the Greeks, as we have seen, it was an open question. Democritus could argue for materialism, and Plato for idealism. The full power of the Christian Church had been mobilized during the Middle Ages against materialism; but the New Science, with its conception of natural law broadened to include the functioning of the human body, was now inviting a return to a materialistic way of thinking. When Descartes faced the problem anew he had to weigh in his balance the authority of traditional religion and the compelling evidence of the new science. The Cartesian solution was a compromise, and one suspects that Descartes was not always as frank as he pretended to be. Nevertheless, he was the first to try seriously to show concretely how mind and body are related. His physiology was primitive, and his psychological analysis was constricted by his logic; but he launched two great movements, one toward the mechanistic interpretation of the functioning of the body, the other toward the introspective analysis of the contents of consciousness.

Descartes' solution to the mind-body problem is, we have noted, that of dualistic interactionism. Mental causes produce physical effects; physical causes produce mental effects. What are the processes whereby one can act causally on the other? Before we examine the answer we must examine Descartes' conceptions of mind and body.

Few thinkers of the seventeenth century could be expected to dispute openly the orthodox Christian conception of the soul as separable and immortal. There might be disagreements as to its location in the body, as to its degree of rationality, as to its destiny after the death of the body, and so forth, but the conception was so deeply rooted in the culture of the time as to be simply taken for granted. Descartes may have been secretly a heretic, but openly he professed himself a devout Roman Catholic. What he did was propose a method of inquiry which if followed rigorously could never impair, but only strengthen, one's faith. The Cartesian method is the method of universal doubt. Only that can be really believed which, when doubted, carries within itself the assurance of its own indubitability. This was not original with Descartes; centuries before, St. Augustine had insisted on the same test of truth. Descartes was the first in modern times, however, to present it systematically as a method; and it is to Descartes that we trace the origins of the introspective movement in modern psychology.

To follow the Cartesian method is, as Descartes put it, to strip oneself of all past beliefs, to place all the data of experience in question, to examine these data without bias and to make what inferences one can from this fresh scrutiny of the data. The data are, of course, the facts of consciousness; for even the belief in the existence of a physical world has been temporarily suspended. If we follow this procedure, Descartes argued, we find that some facts are presented so "clearly and distinctly as to exclude all ground of doubt." From these "clear and distinct" impressions we then deduce the logical consequences. The Cartesian method is thus *empirical,* in the sense that it begins with the unbiased observation of experience, but also *rational,* since the initial observations are replaced by rational deductions. During the later history of psychology it was the "rationalism" of the Cartesian method that survived. His insistence on the introspective analysis of consciousness did not become central in psychology until the late nineteenth century.

We cannot here reproduce Descartes' ingenious justification of a belief in God and in the laws of physical nature. Suffice it to say that for Descartes the first indubitable fact of introspection is the fact that the very act of doubting reveals the existence of a doubter. *Cogito ergo sum* (I think, hence I am) has become almost a slogan for the Cartesian argument. Just as the fact of thinking carries its own proof of the existence of a *res cogitans* (something that thinks), so the evident imperfection of thought compels one to believe in a Perfect Being who created not only the thinker but also the object of his thought, namely, a material world that behaves in accordance with divine law. The Cartesian doctrine gives us a conception of mind as a thinking substance, essentially different from matter, in which God has planted certain ideas (innate ideas), like the idea of God itself, which are essentially indubitable. In this respect Descartes was a thoroughgoing Platonist.

By virtue of his method, however, Descartes was able to affirm the existence of a material world that is governed by law. He was thus free, without renouncing his belief in God, to explore the laws of nature as they were being revealed by the new science. His curiosity about nature led him into mathematics and physics, and he even contemplated a comprehensive treatise on all knowledge analogous to that of Aristotle. It is his physiology, however, that interests us here. During Descartes' lifetime physiology was becoming a science. The theories of Galen were being called into question; Harvey's new interpretation of the circulatory mechanism (1628) was exciting comment; the time was ripe for a new interpretation of bodily functions in thoroughly naturalistic terms.

Descartes was by no means the most creative physiologist of his day; he made no great discoveries, and he even failed to appreciate the full significance of Harvey's theory. Nevertheless, his system was a brilliant attempt to interpret all the functions of the body in terms of the mechanical laws of cause and effect. We must be content with an illustration from his analysis of the sensory-motor functions. The sense organs are affected by motions in the external world. Operating like bell-wires, the sensory nerves open valves in the brain to which they are attached, thereby permitting the animal spirits, stored in the "central cavity" (ventricle) of the brain, to flow through the motor nerves to the muscles, producing an appropriate flexion of the muscles. The animal spirits are not the immaterial *pneuma* of Galen but fine material particles in the blood which seep through the arteries into the central ventricle. The total response is thus a self-contained mechanical cause-effect sequence, requiring the assumption of no immaterial agency. He referred to it as "reflected motion," and we are tempted to see in this an anticipation of the modern conception of the reflex.

This is very primitive physiology. What is important, however, is the fact that he was honestly trying to explain the functioning of the body in terms of the laws that were being formulated by the new scientists. Since the time of Descartes nearly all of his specific theories have been discarded, but his faith in the ultimate intelligibility of bodily functioning in terms of natural law has been maintained.

But Descartes had to reconcile his mechanistic physiology with the "indubitable" facts of introspection; he had to show how mind and body could be causally interactive. Here his theorizing was less fortunate. He could assert with equanimity that animals are complete automata, for to believe that animals have souls would be contrary to Christian doctrine. To assert that the human body is an automaton, however, and at the same time to accept the apparently obvious fact that the mind has some degree of control over the body, is to place oneself in a dilemma. Either the material world is not a self-sufficient system or else the "indubitable" fact of human freedom is merely an illusion, a dilemma which called into question either one's scientific or one's religious faith. Descartes' solution of the problem is far from convincing. In the early seventeenth century the law of conservation of energy had not yet been clearly formulated, but there was something like a "law of conservation of motion". Motion, most scientists believed, could be transmitted from one body to another but could not in any absolute sense be created or destroyed. The functioning of the body, Descartes argued, is regulated by the motions of the animal spirits. Since the animal spirits belong to the material world their motions cannot be created by an immaterial cause. But how about the *directions* of their motion? Descartes' unsatisfactory theory was that while the mind cannot produce motions in the animal spirits it can determine their direction. It is as though at any point of choice the mind could switch the motion from one track to another without increasing or decreasing it. If Descartes had had the benefit of Newton's analysis of the laws of motion he would have realized that any change of motion, even in its direction, requires the application of force.

Even less satisfactory was Descartes' theory as to where the interaction between mind and body takes place. Since the mind is an "unextended substance" it obviously cannot have a precise location in the body. The body, however, is a part of the material world, so it would seem plausible that the interaction must take place through some organ of the body, principally in the brain. For reasons that bear no relation to any relevant facts Descartes selected the pineal gland as the point of interaction. Apparently he was impressed by the fact that, whereas most of the structures of the brain have their symmetrical opposites, this particular organ stands alone. We may note with relief that this particular theory has never found support, even from the most ardent of Cartesians.

The facts which invite an interactionist theory are obviously hard to resist; but equally obviously the theory runs afoul of the law of conservation of energy. If energy is physical, and if mental acts produce physical changes, then either the mind is a part of physical nature or else there is a special "mental" energy that does not conform to physical law. Even before the concept of energy was clearly formulated the difficulty was recognized. The whole trend of the new science was against the assumption that the laws of nature are not self-sufficient; yet the facts of observation seemed to demand a dualism of mind and body. One resolution of the problem was the doctrine of psychophysical parallelism, propounded first by Descartes' Belgian pupil Geulincx (1625–1669) and later systematized by Leibnitz (1646–1716). Geulincx was responsible for the famous "two clock" analogy. Let us assume that we have two clocks, set to indicate the same time and operating without error. If one strikes the hour and the other does not, an observer watching the hands of the nonstriking clock and hearing the other strike at the appropriate time will conclude that there is a causal relationship between the two. Mind and body, said Geulincx, are like two perfect clocks which God wound up and set going. The impression that an act of will causes a motion in the body is an illusion, due to the coincident operation of two sets of parallel laws, one mental and one physical.

At first glance, this theory seems even more ridiculous than the theory of interaction. It requires a conception of God as a sort of I.B.M. monster, and it leaves unanswered a multitude of questions raised by such phenomena as dreams, hallucinations, delusions and even simple errors of judgment; God's clocks are supposed to keep perfect time. Also, it strains our faith to believe that sometime, somewhere, one of the clocks will not go wrong, the amusing consequences of which tickle the imagination. It cannot be said that Leibnitz lent clarity to the parallelist theory; but he undoubtedly gave it dignity by clothing it with an imposing system of meta-physics. The details of his metaphysics need not concern us. He was a monist in the sense that he believed in a single all-pervasive God, a pluralist in his belief in an infinite number of soul-units, or monads, a parallelistic dualist in his assertion that everything that appears to be physical has its mental correlate.

The Monadology of Leibnitz now reads almost like a fairy tale. He postulated an infinite number of monads, each with its own con-sciousness, each in its own modest way mirroring the whole universe, no one monad having a causal relationship with any other monad, the actions of all monads harmonized in accordance with a divine plan, all monads organized in a hierarchy, the supreme monad being the human soul. Instead of two clocks Leibnitz postulated an infinite number of clocks, all ticking together, all keeping perfect time. The doctrine of pre-established harmony, with its implication that we are living in "the best of all possible worlds" was brilliantly satirized in Voltaire's "Candide," with Professor Pangloss representing Leibnitz. Bertrand Russell, one of the best of the modern Leibnitzian scholars, suggests that Leibnitz in his Monadology was something less than candid in the presentation of his real philosophy; Leibnitz was dependent on court favors for his living, providing solace to defend-ers of the status quo. Presumably Russell is right; but it was the published works of Leibnitz rather than his private thoughts that affected early modern psychology.

Fanciful as the Monadology would appear to be we find that, stripped of its imagery, it has provided a framework within which many subsequent psychologists have been content to work. In fact, at least one contemporary psychologist (cf. L. T. Troland, *The Mystery of Mind*,) has tried to reconcile it with the best evidence of modern neurophysiology. An interactionist theory is simply too difficult to accept, although even this type of theory has also had its recent defenders (cf. Wm. McDougall, *Body and Mind*). A parallelist theory has at least the virtue that it can affirm a relationship between mind and body without necessarily being tied down to any particular metaphysical explanation of that relationship. Thus many psycholo-gists have been willing to assert, without hazarding an explanation, that for every mental process there must be a corresponding process in the nervous system, and have proceeded from this assumption to the establishment of psychophysical and psychophysiological correlations. This is clearly an assumption that can at least in part be tested by observation. Few, however, have been willing to make the companion assumption that for every physical (or even neural) process there must be a corresponding mental process. Such an hypothesis is untestable, and will remain so until we develop methods of observing unconscious mental processes. So long as we maintain a dualism of the mental and the physical, it may be that parallelism is the most convenient type of theory.

For Leibnitz, however, and for Spinoza before him, the doctrine of parallelism was not a mere convenience; it was an essential part of a metaphysical theory. Spinoza had answered Descartes by asserting that the mental and the physical are merely two of an infinite number of attributes of a Supreme Being. The orderliness of nature and the correspondence between the facts of nature and our perceptions of them are evidences of the unity of God. Spinoza's concerns were mainly ethical and theological, and he did not give us a concrete psychophysiological theory. Leibnitz, the mathematician, was more precise. Each monad, he asserted,—and this means each infinitesimal particle of the universe—is possessed of consciousness, is capable of perception. The *petites perceptions* of the little monads are organized into the *apperceptions* of the soul-monads. This is a panpsychic doctrine, reminiscent of the Neo-Platonists. It implies that what we call "mental" is so rooted in reality that we shall find it expressing itself everywhere. Although tradition has labeled Leibnitz as a dualist, we find in his psychophysical parallelism an expression of a faith that at bottom the laws of mind and the laws of matter are one.

For the psychologist, three of the foregoing points must be underlined. In the first place, the Leibnitz theory required a mental determinism analogous to the determinism of the physical sciences. There must be psychological law analogous to physical law; and the two sets of laws must correspond. The Scholastics had believed in a "mental" law, but it bore no relation to the laws of nature. For Leibnitz and for Spinoza, the laws of God are universal. The Leibnitzian psychology was thus just as deterministic as was the contemporary Newtonian physics. In the second place, Leibnitz introduced the conception of unconscious mental processes. The *petites perceptions* of the little monads were not conscious, in the sense that they were not recognizable as such in the *apperceptions* of the soul-monad, but they were nevertheless important. Herbart, von

Hartmann and Freud were later to make much of the doctrine of the unconscious. Leibnitz permits us to carry the principle of mental determinism beyond the limits of the directly observable contents of consciousness. And thirdly, and perhaps this is a corollary, Leibnitz's theory reaffirms and broadens the Cartesian conception of innate mental structure. We shall later be able to appreciate the enormous importance of this conception in psychological theory.

The explicitly monistic theories that found favor in the early modern period are typified by the subjective idealism of Berkeley and the materialism of La Mettrie. Berkeley's idealism is of more interest to the philosopher than it is to the psychologist. It provides delight, and frustration, for every beginning student of philosophy, for Berkeley leads us gently and inexorably to the conclusion that the material world has no existence as such but is merely a set of ideas in the mind of God. After our initial confusion, however, we discover that it really makes no difference so far as the mind-body problem is concerned; for Berkeley merely reinstated as different types of idea the old-fashioned distinction between mind and matter, *i.e.,* ideas that seem to have "mental" attributes and ideas that seem to have "physical" attributes. The problem of relating the two remains unchanged. Indeed, as we shall see, Berkeley proposed a theory of vision which is as "hard-boiled" as that of any materialist.

The challenge of La Mettrie's materialism was, by contrast, more to the scientist than to the philosopher. Brushing aside the traditional theological doctrine of the soul, and its justifications by the philosophers, he boldly asserted that the soul is nothing more than the thinking part of the body, that it lives and dies as such, and that it operates in accordance with physical law. There is no reason, consequently, why all the phenomena that have been called "mental" cannot be fully explained in mechanistic terms. La Mettrie was extending the Cartesian mechanism to include the "off bounds" territory that Descartes had reserved for the mind. The nimble philosopher is usually able to evade such an attack. The theologian strikes back with denunciations; and La Mettrie was roundly denounced. For the scientist, however, it was an invitation. Newton had conquered the physical world, and the anatomists and physiologists were explaining the functions of the body in naturalistic terms. La Mettrie was not a good scientist himself, but his enthusiasm was contagious. By the middle of the eighteenth century some scientists, especially in

England and France, were beginning to entertain the thought that all mental phenomena might eventually be explained as natural facts.

At the end of the eighteenth century the mind-body problem was still essentially metaphysical; but we have seen how the metaphysicians were attempting to cope with the facts of the new science. If they were not revising their theories in the light of the facts, they were at least struggling to find facts to fit their theories. The relevance of facts of observation was beginning to be appreciated. The time was ripe for a new scrutiny of the facts. During the next hundred years, as we shall see, the relation between mind and body, while still a problem for the philosophers, gradually became subjected to the discipline of science. The eighteenth century leaves us with the mind-body problem still unresolved; but the problem was beckoning to the scientist, inviting him to the arduous but enthralling task of building theory out of fact.

THE NATURE OF COGNITION

Cognition is the process whereby we attain knowledge. Whether or not we can attain true knowledge is, as we have seen, one of the persistent problems of philosophy. The Greeks faced the problem from every point of view, and tended to come out with a rationalistic solution. The mediaeval Christians accepted Greek rationalism within the context of a doctrine of divine revelation. The new science revived the misgivings of Protagoras, and led men to question again the authority of reason and revelation. Can it be that what we think we know is but a set of probability statements, built with gradually increasing stability on the foundation of facts of observation? In the spirit of the new science the philosophers of the seventeenth century began for the first time to examine the processes of cognition as the scientists were examining the motions of natural bodies. We cannot claim that the early modern theories of cognition were unsullied by philosophic preconceptions, but we can at least respect their authors for the honesty with which they attempted to suspend their biases.

Any theory of cognition must deal with the problems of sense-perception, memory, imagination and thinking. These are the processes whereby we have knowledge of, or are deceived about, the world of reality. The early modern theories of cognition tend to fall into two categories, the empirical and the rational. The empirical theories were characteristically British—Locke, Berkeley, Hartley, Hume, although the Frenchman de Condillac was fully as empirical as any of these; the rationalistic theories were predominantly Continental—Descartes, Leibnitz, Wolff, Kant, although the Scottish school of Thomas Reid had overtones of rationalism. The divergent trends, which persist to this day, are interesting to the social historian—England and America, struggling toward a democratic way of life, looking to experience; the Continental countries still, except for the Netherlands, in the grip of monarchies, searching for absolutes. For us the comparison must be between theories rather than between forms of government. On both sides of the English Channel philosophers were challenged by the problem of cognition.

THE EMPIRICAL APPROACH AND THE EMPIRICAL THEORY

Empiricism can have two meanings. On the one hand, it may represent a disposition to demand a scrutiny of the facts of experience before any theory is propounded. We may call this an *empirical approach.* In this sense, Descartes was an empiricist, as was Locke. On the other hand, we have the *empirical theory,* the theory that all contents of the mind, without residue, are derived from experience. In this second sense Descartes was not an empiricist, for he believed in the innateness of certain ideas. Locke was almost an empiricist, but his theory is muddied by certain statements about the "powers" of the mind. Condillac (1715–1780) might be considered the complete empiricist in that, in his fantastic analogy of the statue that was suddenly endowed with olfactory sensitivity, he tried to demonstrate that one set of sensory impressions could lead through associative processes to the recreation of the whole perceptual world; but the Condillac analysis, delightful as it is, bears no reference to any demonstrable fact. It is in the writings of the Scotsman David Hume that we find the most stubborn attempt of modern times to develop a complete and consistent empirical theory.

The German language provides a useful distinction between two meanings of the word "experience." *Erlebnis* refers to that which one consciously "lives through" at a given time, as in "The concert was a thrilling experience" or "The blunder I made during the intermission was an embarrassing experience". Experiences, in this sense, can be directly inspected and analyzed. On the other hand, there is *Erfahrung*, or the cumulative result of many past *Erlebnisse*. Thus we may speak of "the experienced diplomat" or of the wisdom that sometimes "comes with experience". Empiricism as an *approach* in early modern psychology represented an interest in *Erlebnisse*, in the conscious experiences of the individual; empiricism as a *theory* was an attempt to explain what we now are in terms of *Erfahrung*, *i.e.*, in terms of the experiences we have had in the past.

The empirical approach was characteristic of the new movement in physical and biological science, and this was reflected in the psychology that was beginning to emerge. The scientists were eager to let Nature speak for herself. The philosophers, with less conviction, were willing to concede that psychological theorizing should be preceded by careful observation of the facts of experience. Their attempts at psychological observation should not be disparaged, however. Descartes' account of his self-analysis as reported in the *Discourse on Method* may not be strictly true, but at least it is a statement of an ideal that was later to come closer to actualization. The British empirical philosophers may not have suspended all their biases, but we find in their writings a multitude of shrewd distinctions that could have come only from the painstaking observation of experience; and we also find in the writings of scientists like Newton a genuine curiosity about such experiences as those of color. Nevertheless, when we speak of the empiricism of seventeenth and eighteenth century psychology our reference is usually to the theory rather than to the approach. Psychology did not begin to become genuinely empirical in its approach until late in the nineteenth century; and even today the two meanings of the word "empirical" are regularly confused.

The empiricist theory is essentially a theory of knowledge, *i.e.*, it is epistemological rather than psychological. The early modern empiricists were defending the thesis that experience is the source of all knowledge, that experience contains its own criteria of truth, that no special process of revelation need be postulated. Empiricism was a radical movement that challenged the authority of revealed religion and affirmed a faith in the adequacy of natural law. We must hasten to note that few of the early empiricists were anti-religious; Locke, for instance, believed firmly in God, and Berkeley was a respected bishop. Their objection was not to religion, but to the doctrine of revelation. Only when the full consequences of empiricism were recognized, as in the writings of David Hume, did it become a real threat to religious faith. The early empiricists had their difficulties with the Church, both Protestant and Roman Catholic, but their real difficulties were political. Empiricism was a challenge, not only to religion, but also to the established social order. The philosophers of the early modern period—Locke, Voltaire, Hume, and others—kept shuttling back and forth across the English Channel in search of a more hospitable climate. To defend an empiricist philosophy required a considerable amount of courage.

Any epistemological theory requires a psychology of cognition. Locke, Berkeley, Hume and Condillac were trying to find *natural* laws of knowing that were in accord with the natural laws of the physical sciences. The search for a naturalistic account of cognition required an examination of cognitive content and cognitive development. The titles of some of the great books of this period reflect the current interest in the cognitive problem, like Locke's *Essay Concerning Human Understanding* (1690), Condillac's *Essai sur l'Origine des Connoissances Humaines* (1746), and Hume's *Enquiry Concerning the Human Understanding* (1748). Each author was attempting to identify the processes whereby we come to know what we know, *i.e.*, to write a psychology of cognition; but each author also hoped through his psychological analysis to solve the broader problems of epistemology.

Two big questions commanded the interest of the early modern empiricists: (1) Is the human mind furnished at birth with certain ideas that could not possibly be learned through experience? This is the problem of innate ideas, posed by the whole rationalist tradition, but especially by Descartes. (2) Can we distinguish between ideas that correctly represent the "real" world from those that are generated by the perceiver? This is a question that goes back to Protagoras, but which became acutely important again with the rise of the new science. In the terminology of John Locke it became the problem of "primary" and "secondary" qualities. The two questions cannot really be kept separate.

But, first, a note about the concept of "idea". At best it is a vague word that has been used with varied meanings and that has been, quite justifiably, excluded from the technical vocabulary of contemporary psychology. After Locke's *Essay,* however, it became part of the standard psychological jargon. The "idea" was the unit of mental content, analogous to the material elements that the physical scientists were discovering. The French writers used the equivalent term *idée.* The Germans could speak of *Ideen,* but they usually preferred the Germanic *Vorstellung,* a word which was later translated back into English as *presentation.* The *idea* (or *idée,* or *Vorstellung*) could be the percept of a tree, the memory of a dead friend, the image of a fictitious centaur or the concept of infinity. In Locke's language an idea is "whatsoever is the object of the understanding when a man thinks." Just as the material world was being broken down into its component elements, so the world of mind could be broken down into its component ideas. In retrospect, we can see that the "idea" was a logical artifact—and future historians may pass the same judgment on the currently popular conceptions of "stimulus" and "response"—but for the early modern empiricists the "ideas" were the building blocks with which mental life was constructed.

Are there any innate ideas? The answer of the empiricists was an emphatic "no." The empiricists represent the "tough-minded" tradition in psychology, a tradition which has maintained itself in England and in the United States. (It was William James, America's greatest philosopher-psychologist, who distinguished between tough-minded and tender-minded psychologies). Thomas Hobbes was probably the first of the tough-minded British empiricists; but it was John Locke who gave the empiricist theory its clearest formulation. Descartes had asserted that the ideas of the self, of God and of the spatial and temporal dimensions of the material world are firmly implanted in the mind of man, *i.e.,* that these are prior to individual experience and are known directly by intuition. Locke countered with the assertion that there are no ideas in the mind of man that were not derived from sense perception. *Nihil est in intellectu quod non fuerit antea in sensu.* Locke's analysis in his *Essay* was a brave attempt to demonstrate that if we are to understand human mentality we need not assume a determining mental structure. For him the mind was a *tabula rasa,* a blank sheet on which anything could be written. (The analogy was to the wax tablet that the Romans used which, after the writing, could be scraped down to present a smooth surface.) Restated in terms of contemporary jargon, Locke's assertion was that the principles of "learning" will explain all of what we know and what we are.

As a matter of fact, Locke was not completely consistent. While he rejected the Cartesian doctrine of innate ideas he made frequent reference to the "powers" and "faculties" of the mind, implying thereby that the mind is an entity that can operate under its own steam. It required the relentless logic of David Hume to demonstrate, a century later, that if the empiricist principle is fully accepted Mind must be regarded as a phantasm with no real existence. Nevertheless, Locke's empiricism, however faulty, was destined to burgeon into a doctrine of man that was to dominate British and American psychology for nearly three hundred years.

John Locke's influence mounted rapidly after the publication of his *Essay,* and continued to spread for a century after his death; but his theories had at times rough going. He could dispose, to the satisfaction of many, of the doctrine of innate ideas; the temper of the times was against the assumption that the human mind was not self-sufficient. He encountered difficulties, however, when he tried to give an epistemological and psychological reply to the challenge of the new science. The new science, while affirming its faith in the absoluteness of natural law, was reviving Protagorean doubts about the dependability of sense perception. Does the naked eye necessarily tell us the truth, for instance, when the microscope gives us a quite different picture? Do the colors of the rainbow correspond to something really there in the physical world? The physicists were reducing the world to terms of space, time, mass, force and motion; but where in the world of the physicist can we find the colors, sounds and smells of sensory experience? The physicist's reduction of these to motions of material particles threatened to relegate sensory qualities to the realm of illusion. Locke's resolution of the problem was far from satisfactory. In fact, there are some who regard his doctrine of primary and secondary qualities as one of the more pernicious errors in the history of cognitive theory. Right or wrong, however, it set the pattern for much of subsequent cognitive psychology and, in garbled form, it is still with us. If only for this reason, it deserves closer inspection.

In his epistemology Locke was a representative realist, *i.e.,* he believed that there is a real world, that exists independently of our knowing it, and that is more or less faithfully represented in our experience of it. Where the representation is correct, we have knowledge; where it is incomplete we have error. The task of the epistemologist is to determine criteria whereby the representation can be judged as correct or incorrect. The real world is the world revealed by the physical sciences, but the representation of this in experience is sometimes distorted by factors inherent in the perceiver. This is a simple and appealing theory, and one is not astonished at its perennial popularity.

Representative realism obviously demands a psychology of cognition, and such a psychology Locke tried to develop. Stated in the simplest possible way, his question was: How much of the content of consciousness is contributed by the real world, and how much by the perceiver? During the rest of our survey we shall see how this business of parcelling out determinants has proved to be a continuing source of confusion. For Locke, however, the answer was clear. The material world contains nothing but space, time, mass, force and motion. (Newton's *Principia* preceded Locke's *Essay* by only a few years.) When we perceive an object we always perceive it as extended in space, enduring in time, having a certain degree of substantiality, and so forth; and even when we subdivide it we perceive the same basic qualities. These are the *primary* qualities of perception, which correspond to the primary characteristics of the real world, and they are reflected directly in consciousness. On the other hand, there are the "sensory" qualities, like colors, sounds and smells, which seem to vary with the conditions of observation and the state of mind of the perceiver. The snowdrop may look white to the naked eye, but through the microscope it may show all the colors of the spectrum. One is tempted to conclude that the sensory qualities are *secondary*, determined not by the thing itself but by the perceiver.

Now it is obvious that any object of knowledge contains secondary as well as primary qualities. Locke's judgment was that the primary qualities are the qualities inherent in nature, the dimensions of the real world that the physicists were measuring, and that these are directly and correctly represented in consciousness. The secondary qualities are contributions of the perceiving mind. In this way Locke made his peace with the new science of nature. There are hints in his writings that quality may eventually be restated in terms of quantity, but in his day the ghost of the Mind as an entity could not yet be exorcised.

Locke's further theory is less challenging, but it is interesting from the point of view of subsequent history. Accepting as fact the origin of all primary ideas as contributions of the senses, he still had to account for the superstructure of thought. After all, people remember, imagine and conceptualize; mental life is much more than what is here and now and actual. Locke solved the problem by assuming that simple "ideas of sense" could generate "ideas of reflection," and that these could be combined in an infinite number of ways to produce the abstract world of thought. He did not, in fact, revive all the Aristotelian laws of association, although he might well have done so. What we owe to John Locke is the simple and pure conception of human mentality as capable of dissection into its constituent ideas, some simple, some complex, all bound together in accordance with empirically determinable laws. Each individual possesses a unique combination of mental contents, as distinctive as are the features of the face—hence the fact of individuality; but all these mental contents (ideas) are facts that are accessible to observation and that can be subsumed under general laws.

We have noted that Locke's empiricism was not complete. He was neither completely empirical in his approach, for his "ideas" were constructs rather than data; nor was he consistently empirical in his theory, for he did not satisfactorily refute the Cartesian doctrine of innate ideas; the notion of a priori mental structure can always be found lurking behind his arguments. Nevertheless, the Locke who is known to the history of psychology is the man who asserted that the contents of the human mind can be observed, analyzed and explained in accordance with natural principles. With Locke, psychology was beginning to find a place for itself in the new science.

Locke's contemporaries and successors were far from gentle with him. Berkeley, Hume and de Condillac agreed with his rejection of innate ideas, but insisted on a much more rigorous refutation of the doctrine; and Berkeley was particularly cruel in his critique of the distinction between primary and secondary qualities. The Continental Rationalists, led by Leibnitz, scorned the whole empirical philosophy as utterly superficial and inadequate. Locke did not live to face his major critics, but it is a tribute to his greatness that we still read his book as the classic of modern empiricism.

Berkeley's argument against Locke was essentially epistemological. At the age of 24 Berkeley had published a thoroughly empiricist theory of space perception. A year later his *Principles* appeared, presenting his defense of the doctrine of subjective idealism. His most direct attack on Locke came after three more years when in his *Three Dialogues Between Hylas and Philonous* he reduced the doctrine of representative realism to an absurdity. Without challenging the empiricist position he argued with a logic that is difficult to refute that our ideas of extension, duration, motion, etc. (the primary qualities) are just as dependent on the perceiver as are those of color, sound and smell. In other words, all qualities of perception, primary as well as secondary, are dependent on the perceiver. *Esse est percipi* (to be is to be perceived) became the slogan of a subjective idealism that denied the distinction between the world of mind and the world of matter. For philosophy this was an important step, for it represented the first consistent idealistic monism of modern times. For psychology, as we have noted, it meant very little. As an idealist Berkeley asserted that the physical world can have existence only as an array of ideas in the mind of the observer. As an observer of nature he could not deny the fact that there seems to be a natural order that is resistant to the whims of the observer. He had consequently to conclude that a superordinate Divine Mind encompasses both types of idea, physical as well as mental. He thus reinstated, within the framework of idealism, all the facts and problems that had previously invited a dualistic theory. Apart from his brilliant, if possibly erroneous, theory of space perception, Berkeley's contribution to psychology lies mainly in his destruction of the distinction between primary and secondary qualities. This, we shall see, was quite important for nineteenth century theory.

Hume's theory of cognition follows logically as well as historically after that of Berkeley, but it represents a much broader conception of the problem. Born and bred in Calvinist Scotland, he spent many of his creative years in the "enlightened" France of Voltaire, Diderot and Rousseau. He was neither an ecclesiastic nor a professor, and his style of thought and expression was consequently free from pedantry. David Hume was probably the most brilliant of the British empiricists. One of the great tributes to him was from Immanuel Kant, who declared that Hume "awoke him from his dogmatic slumbers."

Hume looms large in the history of all psychological thought. Our interest at this point is merely in his theory of cognition. Historians of philosophy sometimes classify him as a sceptic, although it is certain that he was not a sceptic in the strict sense of the term. Hume was never sceptical, for instance, about the rules of inference. He tried to explain these rules psychologically, but he used them in his explanation. What is important is that he attempted for the first time to develop a completely empirical theory of cognition on the basis of a consistently empirical approach. The fact that neither his approach nor his theory proved to be consistently empirical need not detract from the merit of his effort. No psychologist has ever succeeded in being completely and consistently empirical.

If we reject, with Locke, the doctrine of innate ideas and, with Berkeley, the distinction between primary and secondary qualities, what have we left? We are left with nothing but an ordered array of mental contents. How explain the order? To introduce a Divine Mind as an ordering agent was for Hume a cowardly way out, although Hume did not deny the existence of God; and to explain order in terms of a partially represented physical world that is itself ordered appeared to be a mere begging of the question. The true empiricist, Hume believed, must find the explanatory principles *within* experience itself. In other words, the psychologist must first look at the data of experience before he attempts to set up explanatory constructs. Hume had no quarrel with Descartes' method of universal doubt, but he considered as hasty and unwarranted many of Descartes' inferences.

The raw data of experience for Hume were pretty much what Locke called "ideas". According to Hume, however, we must accept these just as they appear, without making any assumptions about their origin. Some of these mental contents appear as vivid and compelling, like the tree I bump into or the thunderclap that startles me; these Hume called "impressions". Others are less vivid, like the memory of the tree or of the thunderclap; for these, Hume reserved the term "idea". The essential difference between an impression and an idea, however, is merely that impressions are tougher, stronger, more vivid than are ideas. Memory, for example is merely "faded sense". Mental contents present dimensions of variation like extension, duration and vividness, but these are dimensions rather than absolute categories.

Hume's greatest challenge, however, was to the rationalistic doctrine of mental structure. Descartes and Leibnitz had maintained that the mind had its own structure, and even Locke had conceded to the mind certain "powers" and "faculties". Hume was not ready to reduce all mental laws to laws of nature, but he was willing to push the empirical principle to its limits. Descartes had argued that the very fact of thinking demonstrates the existence of a thinker, i.e., a self. But what, asked Hume, is the self? Is there in experience a single, continuous entity that can be called a self? Hume's answer was "no." Our feelings of "selfhood" change from percept to percept. The "self" is merely an abstraction from a great many particular experiences. The same holds true for our ideas of God and of the material world. In modern terminology these ideas are not data but constructs. The thoroughgoing empiricist, Hume believed, can accept only those constructs (ideas) that are unequivocally representative of primary sensory impression.

One of the toughest problems for the empiricist has always been the problem of causation. If all knowledge comes through the senses, through what senses is the notion of causality conveyed? The Newtonian world is unintelligible without the assumption of cause-effect relationships among its material elements. The challenge to the empiricist was to explain, without the postulate of a superordinate rational principle, how it is that we apprehend the world in terms of causal relationships. In this connection Hume presented one of his boldest and most controversial theories. The elementary impressions of sense, he claimed, include in themselves no impression of causality. Sensory impressions are ordered in space and time, but there is nothing in immediate experience to indicate that because B follows A therefore B is caused by A. We apprehend A as causing B only after we have repeatedly observed that A preceded B. The notion of causality is thus, in the last analysis, nothing more than a sort of mental habit.

The metaphysical consequences of such a theory are obviously rather disturbing, for it suggests that in the apparently necessary connections in nature—and, by the same token, in the axioms of mathematics and logic—we have nothing but a set of mental habits. With a different array of experiences behind us we might conceivably have arrived at a completely different, and equally undependable, conception of the universe. We have noted that Hume's scepticism was not consistent, but we can readily understand the threat he presented to the rationalistic tradition. Hume was trying to develop a theory of knowledge based exclusively on psychological analysis.

Whether or not he succeeded is debatable, but at least he has the merit of having tried. Hume was hailed by the philosophers of the Enlightenment, and was damned by the rationalists. Much of the psychology of the succeeding century was an attempt to develop further or to escape from the consequences of his analysis.

THE RATIONALISTIC APPROACH

Rationalism in psychology goes back to Plato, but particularly to Aristotle's doctrine of the "rational soul" as something over and above the nutritive and sensory functions of the individual. To be a rationalist, in this sense, is to believe in a special mental substance which possesses its own inherent properties and which cannot be reduced to terms of matter. The doctrine of the rational soul was kept alive during the Middle Ages by the Christian theologians although, as we have noted, their concern about the soul's destiny tended at times to becloud their interest in its nature and attributes. It is intelligible that, as the new science steadily extended its domain, the theologians should cling more and more passionately to the belief that at least the soul of man cannot be boxed in by natural law, and that rational psychology should become one of their last defenses against materialism.

It would be unfair to the rationalists, however, to regard them merely as the brave defenders of a losing cause. Descartes was imbued with the spirit of the new science. He tried honestly, we believe, to apply the methods of science to the analysis of consciousness; and he came to what was for him the inescapable conclusion that the laws of mind cannot be subsumed under the laws of matter. There is, he believed, a *res cogitans*, a thinking substance, that belongs in a different realm of reality. He tried to be empirical, and he concluded that the empirical approach requires something more than an empirical theory. The same is true for Leibnitz. Leibnitz was less interested in empirical observation than was Descartes but, in reply to Locke's assertion that there is nothing in the mind that was not previously in the senses, he was forced to add "*nisi intellectus ipse*—unless it be the mind itself." Descartes and Leibnitz may not have been orthodox Aristotelians, but they believed in the reality of a nonmaterial rational principle that reveals itself in the facts of experience.

What is the modern case for rationalism? For a generation after Leibnitz the banner was carried by a German philosopher, Christian von Wolff (1679–1754), whose *Psychologia Rationalis* (1734) became the accepted eighteenth century exposition of the rational psychology. Wolff was a meticulous scholar in the best German tradition, who spelled out the philosophy of Leibnitz in simple and convincing language, and whose restless energy led him to grapple with all the problems of theology and metaphysics.[1] The historians seem to be agreed that Wolff was not a great creative thinker, although his books were extremely influential. Nevertheless he kept alive an alternative to the empiricism that was growing so rapidly in Great Britain and France. The rational psychology of Wolff was a restatement of the "faculty" psychology of the Aristotelians, readjusted to meet the challenge of the new science. The empiricists were asserting that Aristotle's senses were the sole source of knowledge. Wolff replied with a reaffirmation of the existence of the human soul as a simple, active, immaterial substance, possessing its own powers and its own faculties. Faculty Psychology is often derided as little more than the elaboration of classifications, guilty of such circular reasoning as "We are able to remember because we have a faculty of memory." It is true that many of the lesser expositors of Faculty Psychology seem to regard a classification as an end in itself, and that the accusation of circularity is often justified. Nevertheless we must recognize that the Faculty Psychologists were far from blind to empirical fact. Wolff paid close attention to the findings of the empiricists and strove to incorporate them in his system. What he insisted was, following Leibnitz, that classifiable mental activities imply pre-existing mental capacities that are revealed in experience but not created by experience. Faculty Psychology has never denied the importance of observation; it has asserted, merely, that for a full understanding of man we must also have a complete inventory of man's inherent mental capacities. We shall see later that the modern conception of "psychological functions" is not strikingly different from the older conception of "faculties."

---

[1] In 1719 Wolff wrote a book entitled "*Von Gott, der Welt und der Seele des Menschen, auch allen Dingen überhaupt*" (On God, the World and the Human Soul, also Everything-in-General).

Even more important than the classification of mental faculties, however, was the Rationalist insistence on "activity" as an essential characteristic of mental life. The "impressions" and "ideas" of the empiricists were like the static elements of Newton's material world, activated by forces external to themselves. For the Rationalists— Leibnitz, Wolff and their successors—the essential fact about mind is that it generates its own activity. Mind should not be thought of as an array or a succession of inert "ideas," but rather as an entity that possesses its own power. Psychological analysis must reveal not only the static contents of consciousness but also the underlying mental powers.

The rationalist answer to empiricism is thus found in the concepts of "mental structure" and "mental power". Both were admitted, at least by implication, by Locke but explicitly rejected by Hume. It would be a mistake to regard empiricism and rationalism as utterly incompatible alternatives, but in Hume and Wolff we have perhaps the clearest illustrations of the two opposing attitudes toward the study of man. Tough-minded, outward-oriented Hume wanted to make a natural science of the study of consciousness postulating nothing more than would be acceptable to the most rigorous of Newtonians; meticulous, tradition-oriented Wolff could not discard the insights and the arguments of the past, and clung to the Aristotelian scheme. Although in the writings of Wolff there is little of Hume's sparkle, we find in Wolff something that foreshadows two centuries of German psychology, just as we see in Hume the spokesman for the tough-minded Anglo-American school. British and American psychologists have always been, perhaps naively, wary of metaphysics. German psychologists have characteristically linked their problems to persistent problems of philosophy and have accordingly been less ready to accept the limitations of natural science.

CAN WE HAVE A SCIENCE OF PSYCHOLOGY?

The eighteenth century ends with this question. By "science" was meant the sort of objective observation and measurement that was revealing the laws of the physical world. Hume, as the most outspoken of the empiricists, had questioned the very law of causality on which all science rests, and upset both the philosophers and the scientists. Wolff had retreated from the problem asserting that the laws of mind are not derived from experience. It was Immanuel Kant (1724–1804), the little philosopher of Königsberg, who faced the challenge and left psychology in a state of complete uncertainty. According to Kant, Hume aroused him from his "dogmatic slumbers." Bertrand Russell's unkind comment is that Kant "soon invented a soporific which enabled him to sleep again." The dogmatic slumber had been induced in part by the rationalistic psychology of Wolff. The new "soporific" was the philosophy of Transcendentalism which, far from lulling the world to sleep, stirred up a commotion that has not yet subsided. Kant may have felt content with his answer to Hume, but his answer raised new questions that have since then bothered scientists as well as philosophers.

The Kantian doctrine is enormously complex, and has been variously interpreted by his successors. We must restrict ourselves to its implications for psychology. Curiously enough, both Hume's challenge to rationalism and Kant's answer to Hume lead to the same conclusion, namely, that no science of psychology is possible. The amusing fact is that, after Hume and Kant, a science of psychology began to develop.

If we accept as a fact the existence of a rational soul we can have a science of psychology, albeit a deductive science. If we identify the soul as a set of forms or functions of matter, we can have an inductive science of psychology. If, however, we adopt a radically empirical approach, as Hume tried to do, we are left with nothing but an array of sense impressions which, although they may carry feelings of certainty, cannot convey true knowledge. If we are strictly empirical, and if science implies knowledge, we can have no true science of psychology or anything else. This was Hume's challenge. It disturbed Kant, and it is still a disturbing argument.

Kant's answer is equally disturbing. In his ponderous *Critique of Pure Reason* (1781), which is more nearly intelligible in its English translation than it is in the German original, he attacked both Newtonians' and the empiricists' concepts of space and time. The Newtonians had asserted that space and time were absolute properties of the material world. Hume had argued that spatiality and temporality are merely characteristics of sense impressions. Kant's answer was his "transcendental aesthetic." (The Greek meaning of "aesthetic" is "having to do with sensation." Space and time, according to Kant, are neither independent physical realities nor impressions gleaned from sensory experience; they are *a priori* forms of perception, i.e., ways of perceiving that are prior to all experience. We do not learn our concepts of space and time, as the empiricists were contending; we impose spatiality and temporality on the world because these are inherent characteristics of the perceiving process.

It is easy to see how unsettling such an argument might be, both for the comfortable believer in an orderly material universe and for the sceptical empiricist. It denies the absoluteness of two of the fundamental Newtonian realities, space and time; it suggests that a merely empirical analysis of cognition is crudely superficial; and it threatens an attack on some even more fundamental categories. And this, in fact, is exactly what Kant did. In his "transcendental logic" he demonstrated that, just as space and time are *a priori* forms of perception, so there are forms of thinking which the thinker imposes on the world. Causation, for instance, was for the Newtonians a fact of nature, for Hume an impression derived from the repeated experience of succession. Kant argued that causality is an *a priori* category of thinking. If we think, we must think causally, because this is inherent in the thinking process. Similarly with our concepts of plurality, reality, necessity, and so forth. The order that we think we have discovered in nature is really an order imposed on nature by our own perceiving and thinking processes. But how about the "perceiver" and the "thinker"? Are we to explain away the apparent unity of the self, as Hume tried to do, as merely an abstraction from a cluster of impressions and ideas? Kant's answer was to invoke a still further transcendental principle, the "transcendental unity of apperception." Behind and beyond all individual acts of perceiving and thinking we must assume the existence of a unifying agent. With Kant, psychology recovered its mind, and almost its soul.

We cannot here detail the consequences of the transcendental philosophy. Kant was forced to distinguish between two worlds; the world of *phenomena* (appearances) which is the world we apprehend directly within the framework of our forms of perceiving and our categories of thinking; and the world of *noumena* (things-in-themselves), which is never directly knowable, but about which we can make inferences. The natural scientist begins with phenomena, and tries to deduce from them the characteristics of the noumenal world. The philosopher sets up hypotheses about the noumenal world and tests them for logical consistency. The natural scientists, as we shall see, were not particularly upset by Kant's challenge; and a century of German philosophers welcomed it as an excuse for the spinning of fanciful theories about "the ultimate nature of reality" (cf. Fichte, Schelling, Hegel, Schopenhauer). But what about the psychologists?

Kant's challenge to psychology was even more devastating than was that of Hume. Hume had at least left open the possibility of a science that could observe and count sensory impressions and fashion their combinations into laws. Kant challenged the very basis of a science of psychology. If psychology is the study of "the mind", and if every observation and every deduction is an operation of a mind which silently imposes its own categories on that which is being observed, then how can a mind turn in upon itself and observe its own operations when it is forced by its very nature to observe in terms of its own categories? Is there any sense in turning up the light to see what the darkness looks like?

The implication of Kant's philosophy is that no empirical science of psychology is possible, yet Kant's challenge did not in the least diminish the curiosity of scientists about the phenomena of human experience and behavior. The German philosophers may have wandered into grandiose speculation, but the German scientists, and their French and British colleagues, did not permit the cloud of transcendentalism to obscure their vision. During the nineteenth century the hand that adjusted the test tube and the eye that peered through the microscope began to examine the phenomena of mind.

THE NATURE OF HUMAN NATURE

Every philosopher of the early modern period had to wrestle with this problem. Is man inherently bad or good? Is he capable of rational choice? The Hebraic-Christian tradition, with its belief in "original sin," presented man as a sinner whose salvation depends on an external agency, and the Protestant Nonconformists had revived the doctrine of "election" in an even more severe form. The Greek view of man as a rational being, capable of guiding his own course, was beginning to reappear, but one of the dominant themes in the literature of the period was still "man pursued by fate", a theme that is also rooted in the Greek tradition. We must not forget that in the seventeenth and eighteenth centuries the life of a human being was still priced very low. A man could be hanged or transplanted for what would now be considered merely misdemeanor; a woman could be burned as a witch because of a few minor eccentricities; men were "pressed" into military service, and could be flogged to death for a small breach of discipline. There was little in the experience of the "common man" to nourish a feeling of human dignity. Religion assured him a reward in the after-life if he would only be honest and obedient in this life; but this life provided him few rewards.

The theory of human nature that began to emerge, which is really the theory of human motivation, must be understood in the context of the revolt against authority in religion, of the struggle of the monarchical system for survival, of the growing economic inter-dependence of nations, but, above all, of man's dawning appreciation of his own dignity. The history of the period is studded with distinguished thinkers. We shall select as our prototypes only four of these: Hobbes, the last great philosophic defender of the absolute monarchy; Rousseau, the undisciplined idealist who helped to pave the way for the French Revolution; Adam Smith, who translated his theory of human nature into a science of economics; and Jefferson, the practical materialist, who designed a state in which the common man might live with an awareness of his own dignity. All had this in common: that they tried to develop a theory of society based on a theory of human nature.

Thomas Hobbes (1588–1679) is perhaps the most congenial of all to contemporary students of motivation. Hobbes accepted human nature frankly as something built out of primitive selfish impulses. Man inherits certain primary impulses, like hunger, thirst and sex—these are his original nature; and then he rapidly develops certain other impulses, such as the desire for honor and desire for power. These desires are the continuing motivators of his conduct. He fears pain, and tries to avoid it, and he desires anything that promises to gratify his primary impulses. Everything else he does is a compromise between what he fears and what he desires, regulated by the balance between two sets of impulses. Hobbes was an empiricist in his theory of knowledge. In his resolution of the mind-body problem he was a materialist. Both points of view had better contemporary spokesmen.

It is his theory of conduct that gives him an important place in the history of psychology.

During his long life Hobbes witnessed revolutions and counter-revolutions; he saw the depravity of the common people, and he enjoyed the patronage of the rich and powerful; he was persecuted and fawned upon, despised and honored. His reflections on the nature of human nature left him with little to admire. To Hobbes, man was neither the rational being that the Greeks had idealized nor the Child of God that Christianity had depicted; he was a brute creature, fearful of pain, lusting for pleasure, concerned only about himself but willing to compromise with others for the sake of his own survival. Man in his natural state is at war with all other men. He agrees to a government only because a government will provide him protection.

We need not trace the logic that led Hobbes from these premises to a defense of the absolute monarchy. What interests us is that, long before Darwin, he laid down a doctrine of the "original nature of man": man as an animal, governed by primitive impulse, becoming rational only in response to the need for survival. Since the days of Hobbes the terminology has changed. We now have: "instincts", "prepotent reflexes," "primary drives," "basic needs," "the libido," and so forth; but the central theory of human nature is the same.

Jean-Jacques Rousseau (1712–1778) was born nearly a half-century after the death of Hobbes, and into a society that was stirring with social as well as political revolution; yet his theory of human nature has much in common with that of Hobbes. Rousseau was an erratic character, a Calvinist by training, whose interests ranged from musicology to sociology, and whose personal life has been condemned by many moralists; yet he affirmed a distinctive view of human nature which has influenced the subsequent development both of psychological and of educational theory.

As contrasted with the social philosophy of Hobbes, Rousseau's is essentially an optimistic philosophy. Like Hobbes he believed that man has an "original nature", but he held that this original nature is good; it is society that has ruined him Rousseau's conception of Natural Man has often been misinterpreted as an idealization of the Noble Savage, and indeed the picture of the Noble Savage was to be painted many times by novelists (*e.g.*, James Fenimore Cooper, 1789–1851) and was to influence the early anthropologists of the nineteenth century. What Rousseau was really arguing was that man's inherent nature includes not only the primitive individualistic impulses that Hobbes had recognised but also a capacity for identification with the interests of the community. Rousseau conceived of the "general will" of the community as something over and above the will of the individual, through which the individual can attain his maximum self-realization. For Hobbes the "social contract" was a compromise with other individuals, in the interest of self-preservation; for Rousseau it was also a sinking of individuality in communality. It is easy to see how Rousseau's doctrine of man could inspire men like Robespierre and Saint-Just to rebel against a system that denied liberty, equality and fraternity to the common man; but one can also see in his doctrine of the "general will" the seed of the idea of *Volksgemeinschaft* that was later to inspire the German National Socialists.

Rousseau's contribution to psychological theory was twofold: (1) the idea that human nature, if allowed to develop and express itself freely, will of its own accord grow into a full and free personality; and (2) that the natural endowment of man includes the capacity for identification with the larger social group. The individual is thus more than primitive impulse plus acquired socialization; he is in his natural state a social being. The implications of such a doctrine for education and for politics are far-reaching, although at first glance not completely consistent with one another. On the one hand, education should be a liberation of the individual, should permit the individual to express fully what is inherent in him. On the other hand, society must exercise a constraining influence on the individual, fostering only those patterns of behavior that contribute to the good of the group. It would seem that the individual must be allowed complete freedom of development and at the same time yield his freedom to society. The apparent contradiction can be resolved only if we assume, as Rousseau apparently did, that if man is allowed to develop in accordance with his own nature he will freely accept the good of the larger group as the only real good.

Rousseau has been called the father of the romantic movement, the philosopher of democracy and, by his detractors, a muddled pre-Fascist. However we interpret him, he was enormously influential. With Voltaire (1694–1778) he ranks as one of the theoreticians of the French Revolution and even of the American Revolution; Goethe

(1749–1832) and the German Romantics drew heavily on Rousseau's writings; and in the history of educational theory he stands for the doctrine of "free expression" that was later espoused by the disciples of Freud. It may be that we shall have to distinguish between the Rousseau of history and the Rousseau of legend. The legend, however, may often be more important for the history of ideas than is the historical fact. The "legendary" Rousseau, at any rate, stands for a doctrine of human nature that may be regarded as classic. Hobbes and Rousseau defended one common thesis against the rationalists, namely, that human conduct can be traced back to primitive, irrational impulses that spring from man's "original nature". They differed in their interpretation of original nature. For Hobbes it was individualistic, brutish and, we might say, "bad"; for Rousseau it was socially oriented and "good." Original nature as Hobbes conceived it, and as Christian doctrine presented it, was something to be reckoned with but to be curbed and controlled; for Rousseau it was something to be released and nourished. These two major alternatives, with their ethical overtones only partially suppressed, are still with us.

Adam Smith (1723–1790) is usually classified by the historians as the father of modern political economy. In 1776, the year of the American Declaration of Independence, he published *An Inquiry into the Nature and Causes of the Wealth of Nations*, a book that is still considered the best statement of "classical" economic theory. Until the eighteenth century there was little that could rightly be called "economic theory." The concept of property was deeply rooted in western tradition, and "property" still included wives, children and servants as well as land, goods and chattels. The arts and the tricks of commerce were equally well established. Men had traded since the beginning of human history, and trade has always implied a balancing of value against value. What was lacking was an explicit formulation of the underlying theory of economic value.

The Greeks, of course, and particularly Aristotle, had had much to say about the economics of the city state, and the Romans had had to wrestle especially with the economic problems of labor; but it was not until the eighteenth century that the central problems of economics began to be disentangled from those of politics, ethics and religion. Indeed, even today there are only a few stout souls who claim that economics can be an independent science.

By the eighteenth century the interchange of goods and services within and across national boundaries had become so great as to require every ruler, whether or not he realized it, to act in accordance with an economic theory and as to invite every philosopher to provide an economic theory for his ruler. Hobbes, Locke and Hume were in this sense economists, and so was Rousseau, and even Christian Wolff had developed a theory of national wealth. The dominant view in France ("physiocracy"—the government of nature) was that the wealth of a nation resides, in the last analysis, in its soil. Only agriculture is truly productive; its output exceeds by far the input; a healthy nation should foster in every possible way the productivity of its fields. This was obviously a limited view, appropriate to a country that was rich in land but losing in the struggle for overseas colonies. It contained, however, the concept of "natural resources", which might include the products of the mines and the waters as well as of the fields, and it invited a further inquiry into the meaning of national wealth. Adam Smith accepted the invitation.

Smith was a philosopher and psychologist as well as an economist. In 1759 he had published his *Theory of Moral Sentiments,* in which he defended the thesis that man is inherently altruistic (capable of sympathy) as well as egoistic (interested in his own welfare). His theory of human conduct was, thus, more like that of Rousseau than that of Hobbes. When he approached the problems of economics he concluded, consequently, that the wealth of a nation resides not only in the richness of its natural resources but also in the productivity of its people. For him the measure of economic value had to be the amount of human labor involved in production.

Adam Smith's important contribution to psychological theory was his thesis that the economic life of nations must in the last analysis be understood in terms of the nature of man, and that economic policy should be governed by the laws of human nature. His defense of the principle of free trade, buttressed by analyses of the relation between production and consumption, of wages, prices and the distribution of goods, was an expression of his belief that economic behavior is governed by natural law. If people are allowed to work and trade without undue restriction (the *laissez-faire* policy), the laws of nature will guarantee the maintenance of a "natural level" in the economic life of the nation. This is because a nation is composed of human beings whose natural tendencies are to share with one another just as much as they are to operate in accordance with self-interest. Self-regulation within the economic system is thus a consequence of allowing nature to take its course.

It must be admitted that Adam Smith's economic theory does not necessarily follow from, nor does it necessarily imply, the assumption that man is inherently altruistic. His most brilliant interpreter, David Ricardo (1772–1823), the expositor of "classical" economic theory, discarded as irrelevant the conception of man as a creature of sympathy. Ricardo, too, founded his economics on a psychological theory. The only psychological assumption he required, however, was that man behaves in accordance with a cold calculation of future advantages and disadvantages, a principle (enlightened self-interest) that Jeremy Bentham developed as the basis of a whole social philosophy. Ricardo's "economic man" is obviously a fiction; such a man never existed. Nevertheless many reputable economists have argued that, so far as economic prediction is concerned, the desire for gain is the only human motive that need be postulated. We need not here enter into the controversy among the economists. The extreme positions are: (1) that we can have a science of economics that makes only minimal assumptions about human nature, and (2) that no science of economics can be adequate unless it is grounded in a complete psychology of human motivation. Suffice it to say that Adam Smith, and even Ricardo recognized that at least some assumptions about human nature must be made if we are to understand the economic behavior of man. With Adam Smith the scope of psychological inquiry broadened to include a hitherto unexplored field of human behavior.

Thomas Jefferson (1743–1826), architect of the *Declaration of Independence* and third president of the United States, is not often mentioned in histories of psychological thought; yet he deserves an important place as an embodiment, if not as a formal exponent of a way of thinking about human conduct that was characteristic of the New World. Impatient with the notion of absolute authority in any form, firm in his belief that man is free to shape his own destiny, Jefferson expressed in his life as well as in his voluminous writings what had become the characteristic American self-ideal, namely, that of the courageous, self-reliant, ruggedly independent pioneer. The society he tried to shape was to be a society in which the original equality of all men would be explicitly recognized and in which no man would be denied the opportunity to develop his inherent capacities to the full. The *Declaration of Independence* is as interesting to the psychologist as it is to the political scientist.

Jefferson's view of the universe was that of Newton. He believed in God and in a Divine Plan, but he rejected the separation of the laws of God from the laws of nature; God's plan operates *through* nature. His doctrine of man was pretty much that of John Locke, enriched by his years of residence in the France of Voltaire and Rousseau, and by his acquaintance with the vigorous ideas of Thomas Paine (1737–1809). (Paine, a most unpacifistic English Quaker, came to America in 1774 and through his pamphlets and his books spread the doctrine of the "natural" rights of man.) For Jefferson, all men must be considered as having been born with the same natural rights. He wanted to believe, in accordance with Lockian theory, that they were born also with the same natural capacities, but he was bothered by the biblically ordained doctrine of special creation. Why should God have created some men black and others white, and some men obviously inferior in intelligence to others? Why, in fact, should God have created mosquitoes and lice? If Darwin had appeared a century earlier, Jefferson might not have been so puzzled; as it was, he simply made the best of it. God had a purpose in creating the universe. That purpose must be revealed through natural law. It was obviously God's purpose to create diversity for, since no one person can fathom God's whole plan, each individual must represent one partial and unique expression of God's purpose. Locke had said that "each man's mind has some peculiarity as well as his face that distinguishes him from all others." This principle of diversity of aptitude, of function and of opinion within the context of a single purposive order became for Jefferson one of the bulwarks of his theory of democracy.

Jefferson's doctrine of man was simple and, some have suggested, perhaps a trifle naive; but for Jefferson it made sense as a basis on which a good society could be built. What is unique and important about it is not the originality of any of its component ideas—for all had been anticipated many times—but the fact that it seemed to work. The Constitution of the United States, however faulty it may be, was an application of a theory of man to the practical problems of organizing a society; and it seems to have stood the test of time. Another theory might have served as well, and we remember that long ago Plato gave us an alternative, but the fact remains that

Jeffersonian theory was actually tried out in practice, and with considerable success.

Jeffersonian man is not a disembodied soul or mind but a biological organism, a part of physical nature. His feelings and his thoughts are functions of material structures, which can be studied scientifically as we study rocks and plants. Jefferson was deeply impressed by the French physiologist Cabanis (1757–1808), who argued for a close relation between thought and the brain, and in his old age, he hailed the discoveries of Flourens as a final proof of his thesis that mental life is a function of material process. Every individual, of course, as well as every rock and plant and animal, is a partial revelation of God's design, but we must look to the laws of nature to find the explanation. This, then, is a naturalistic view of man, and it follows that the laws of human interaction must likewise conform to the laws of nature. Jefferson did not develop any great sociological theory, but he maintained the faith that the problems of society will yield to the scientific approach.

Much of Jeffersonian theory is, of course, ethical rather than psychological. Accepting the fact of individual difference as necessary for the "economy of nature," he still insisted on the equality of human rights. Recognizing the potency of environmental influences, he still asserted that the individual has the right to free choice, and the capacity for mastery of his environment, thereby leaving the problem of free will versus determinism completely unsolved. Perhaps what is most important is his faith that, since God created diversity, a pooling of diverse backgrounds and diverse opinions must necessarily bring us closer to the truth. At any rate, with or without the theological justification, this is the essence of the Jeffersonian theory of democracy. Man's instincts are naturally good; men are born to different roles, and they are in part shaped by accidental differences in environment; but, if they can pool their interests on an equal basis, the result will be good for all.

The Jeffersonian tradition has been claimed by both of the leading political parties of the United States. And rightly so, for it embodies a belief both in "rugged individualism" and in "social responsibility", both in the "rights of man" and in the "duties of man," both in "diversity of ability and interest" and in "communality of purpose". As contrasted, for instance, with the Marxist doctrine and the Fascist doctrine there can be nothing more "American" than the belief that man is a free, tough, resilient creature, capable of shaping his own world and courageous enough to rebel against anything that he conceives to be wrong. "A little rebellion, now and then," said Jefferson in a letter, "is a good thing, and as necessary in the political world as storms in the physical. . . ."

Jefferson's conception of man may not have been profound, and he probably could not have debated successfully with a Leibnitz, a Hume or a Kant. It was, nevertheless, a tough-minded, pragmatic doctrine that appealed to the new American nation and that has left its imprint on subsequent American psychology. Only a few decades after Jefferson's death Darwin was to provide scientific support for the naturalistic doctrine of man towards which Jefferson was groping. Jeffersonian, and Darwinian, man is a material organism, limited in its endowment but fumbling towards something that has not yet been achieved.

THE PSYCHOLOGICAL LEGACY OF THE EIGHTEENTH CENTURY

The eighteenth century still conceived the problems of psychology as partial problems of philosophy, of a philosophy that was struggling to cope with all sorts of new challenges to the theory of God, man and the universe. During the nineteenth century the philosophic problems were not forgotten, but the scientists were willing to suspend some of the unanswerable questions while they avidly searched for new facts. With the nineteenth century the theory of man began to pass into new hands. While the philosophers scrambled to keep up with scientific discoveries, and to integrate these into the classic doctrines, the scientists were relentlessly uncovering fact after fact about the functioning of the human body, the relation between man and the animals and even the ways in which people behave in different cultures. The spirit of the nineteenth century was empirical and positivistic. If we can only establish the facts, the scientists kept saying, the theories still will take care of themselves. During the nineteenth century the study of man began to be recognized as one of the sciences of nature.

The philosophical psychology of the eighteenth century leaves us with some general questions about human nature that were to haunt the natural scientists. These are:

(1) *Can Science and Religion Be Reconciled?* The scientists were rapidly conquering the realm of physical nature. Could they also conquer the realm of human nature? Or are there truths about man that will forever be inaccessible to the scientific microscope?

Both the Roman Catholic and the Protestant faiths were at one in their resistance to the scientific threat. Some of man's acts and experiences, they conceded, are governed by the laws of nature, but the essence of man, his soul, is governed by the laws of God. By the end of the eighteenth century the battleground for the fight between science and religion had been laid out, but the preliminary skirmishes had not been very bloody. Since the new science was predominantly a physical science, the religionists could readily protect themselves by asserting the limitations of physical science. It was not until a century later, when the biological sciences experienced their great upsurge, that the battle developed into a real war.

(2) *Can the Mind of Man Be Studied Scientifically?* Each in his own way, Hume and Kant had virtually denied the possibility of a natural science of man, Hume by challenging the whole basis of scientific knowledge, Kant by asserting that the human mind can never at the same time be a cognitive agent and the object of cognition. As we shall see, many of the philosophers retreated from the problem, while the scientists plunged ahead with their observations, leaving to the philosophers the embarrassing task of accommodating their theories to a steadily growing body of fact. Hume and Kant were never satisfactorily answered, but the problems they posed have ever since served to stir the curiosity of scientists.

(3) *Can Ethics be Reduced to Psychology?* Can the distinction between good and bad, right and wrong, be validly made solely on the basis of observation and inference? The Greeks had given an affirmative answer. The Church sturdily insisted that the moral judgment must be guided by the will of God. Some of the philosophers were arguing that man is endowed with a special "moral sense" which transcends his reason. By the end of the eighteenth century the scientists were reviving the question, but they were unsure of their ground. It was the old question of free will versus determinism. All the new discoveries of science tended to support a deterministic position, but against these were the weight of tradition and the simple evidence of direct experience.

(4) *Is Mind More Than Its Contents?* The answer to this question, it will be remembered, highlights one of the main differences between the empiricist Locke and the rationalist Leibnitz; and the contrast becomes even more striking when we compare Hume and Kant. The radical empiricist argued that when all mental contents have been analyzed away there is nothing left. The rationalist retorted that even after the most rigorous of empirical analyses there still remain the powers or faculties or principles of organization that constitute the essence of mind. By the end of the eighteenth century the problem was beginning to be reformulated as the problem of nativism versus empiricism. How much of our experience, of tridimensional space for instance, is built up out of elementary impressions, *i.e.,* is learned, and how much is inherent in the perceptual process? Berkeley had presented a bold empiricist answer that is still a challenge. Kant's rationalist answer is equally challenging. During the nineteenth century it was the scientists rather than the philosophers who attempted to solve the problem by observation and experiment. They did not solve it, and we are now inclined to consider it a spurious problem. As we shall see, however, it touched off a series of investigations that helped to transform psychology into a science.

(5) *What Is the Relation Between Mental Process and Bodily Structure and Function?* The interactionist and parallelist theories of the seventeenth century were highly speculative, supported by an anatomy and physiology of the human body that were still quite inadequate. By the end of the eighteenth century the gross anatomy of the human body had been fairly well laid out, and medical scientists were eagerly searching for functional principles on which a science of physiology could be founded. Mechanists like La Mettrie had argued that all mental activity could be explained as a mechanical function of the body, and the scientific world was prepared for a slogan that was to appear later, "no psychosis without a corresponding neurosis," which meant merely that there is no mental state or process that is not accompanied by a corresponding state or process in the nervous system. By the beginning of the nineteenth century, science was ripe for a direct attack on the mind-body problem.

At the same time the radical separation of man from animal was beginning to be questioned. Aristotle had endowed man with a uniquely "rational" soul, and Descartes had echoed Aristotle. The new science was steadily blurring the distinction between plant and animal and between animal and man. The great Darwinian synthesis was still a long way off, but by the end of the eighteenth century the scientists were looking for facts that might establish for man a legitimate place in the natural order.

PART III

Psychology Becomes a Science

5

A Preview of
Nineteenth Century
Developments

THE YEAR 1800 is not a natural dividing point in the history of man's quest for an understanding of himself, but it is convenient. Let us poise ourselves at the year 1800 and look forward. The nineteenth century was to bring: (1) *the industrial revolution,* first in England, later on the European continent, and still later in other parts of the world; (2) *the consolidation of empires*—British, French, Dutch, German, Belgian—with the resultant interest, initially missionary and commercial, in other peoples; (3) *the awakening of new cultures,* notably in the recently consolidated United States of America, but also in other newly colonized areas like Canada, Australia and South Africa; (4) *the emergence of the democratic ideal,* paced by the American revolution, expressed in part in the French revolution, and registered in successive reforms in the British parliamentary system; (5) *the extension of the humanitarian movement,* evident in the opposition to slavery, the battle for the rights of the underprivileged, the broadening of the meaning of missionary activity to include human welfare as well as religious indoctrination; (6) *a continuing secularization of education,* with the result that by the end of the century the great universities of the western world, as well as most of the school systems, were at least nominally free; and, most important from our point of view, (7) *the broadening of the conception of science* to include all that has to do with the life of man. A few of these developments deserve somewhat more detailed comment.

THE INDUSTRIAL REVOLUTION AND ITS CONSEQUENCES

We tend to think of the nineteenth century as the Victorian Era, a static and stuffy period exuding good manners and dominated by a queen whose devastating comment could be "We are not amused." It is true that Britain's sturdy little queen emphasized, and reflected, a respect for social convention that was characteristic not only of British but also of European and American society. But, although the nineteenth century may have been socially stuffy, it was far from static; it was one of the great revolutionary periods in history. This was Britain's century. By the end of Queen Victoria's reign British dominions, colonies, possessions and protectorates were dotted in red over the map of the world, British industry was marketing its products everywhere, and the British Navy was the undisputed "ruler of the waves." The nineteenth century British Empire may be compared with the Roman and Greek Empires of bygone days.

But, although the nineteenth century belongs in a sense to Great Britain, we cannot overlook the developments in other countries, all of which are important for the understanding of man's thinking about himself.

The industrial revolution was born in England's northern counties with the discovery of adjacent coal and iron deposits. Steel could be produced cheaply and exported at a profit. Britain's mastery of the seas enabled her to bring raw cotton from all parts of the world, to be processed in Lancashire and then exported as finished goods. In the English Midlands (Birmingham, Manchester, Leeds, Sheffield) great industrial centers came into being, drawing men, women and children from the villages to work in the factories. Inventions like the steam engine and the power loom speeded the mechanical process, but threatened to reduce the human being to the position of a cog in the machine. More slowly, but with the same inevitableness, the industrial revolution came to Continental Europe. Coal and iron—in Belgium, the Ruhr, the Saar, Silesia—provided the basis for a new industrial culture. Europe became the producer of swords and ploughshares for the world.

The British had lost their thirteen American colonies, but they had consolidated their position in Canada, Africa and Asia, and were extending their control in the West Indies and the islands of the

South Pacific. The British Empire could boast that no sun could ever set without reflecting its rays from a British territory. The French, while clinging to their possessions in the Atlantic and South Pacific areas, were "developing" North Africa; the Germans were exploiting East Africa, and the Belgians the "Congo" area of Central Africa; and the Dutch were "developing" what is now Indonesia. The European nations were becoming empires that drew raw materials from more and more remote areas and required the export of goods, services, and technical skills.

By the end of the nineteenth century Western Europe had ceased to be economically self-sufficient. The farms were still producing grains and livestock, but the growing population demanded more and more food as well as other commodities like coffee, tea, tobacco and cotton that could be produced more cheaply in warmer climates. The industrial revolution was turning Western Europe into a vast system of factories which received raw materials from all parts of the world, processed them and returned them as finished goods. The great empires were becoming economic systems, at the heart of which were industrial centers like London, Paris, Berlin and Amsterdam, where plans were laid and money was banked, and at the periphery of which were the toiling millions who produced the raw materials. Small wonder that the nineteenth century should have witnessed political, economic and social upheavals. Far from being static, it was one of the most turbulent centuries in history.

During the reign of Queen Victoria the British Empire was relatively stable, although there were painful troubles in India, Canada and South Africa, and the British faced the Russians in a fruitless contest in the Crimea. In Western Europe, however, and in the newly consolidated United States, society was reconstructing itself. In 1848, the year of the revolutions, there were upheavals in France, Germany and Italy, all pointed toward a more democratic system. A few years later the American states came to blows with one another, ostensibly and perhaps really, on the issue of the traffic in slaves; but out of the war there emerged a stronger and stabler republic.

It is always difficult to decide what is cause and what is consequence in history, but one feels fairly sure that, just as the scientific revolution of the Renaissance forced man to reconsider his place in the universe, so the industrial revolution of the nineteenth century forced man to reconsider his place in society. The industrial revolution lured people from the land to the factories with the promise of better wages and easier living, and national wealth increased; but the by-products were slums, disease, and human misery. Novelists like Dickens, Kingsley, Hugo and Dostoyevsky painted the picture of human degradation in vivid colors; humanitarians like Wilberforce battled against the slave trade and child labor; and popular philosophers like Jeremy Bentham preached the doctrine that man's goal should be the welfare of all mankind. The nineteenth century doctrine of man brought into focus the problems of man's relations with other human beings. Two interrelated developments need special emphasis: (1) the growth of class consciousness, and (2) the emergence of social democracy.

The industrial revolution disrupted the class structure of society. Age-old tradition had frozen society into classes that were defined in accordance with bloodlines. In descending order of social status were the royalty, the nobility, the gentry, the merchants, and the peasants. Wealth and power were traditionally allied to class, but even where these had been lost "noble birth" could still assure to a family a high position in society. The industrial revolution upset the system. The merchant class became the great class of entrepreneurs, the developers of new processes, the manufacturers and distributers of goods, the accumulators of wealth and, eventually, the wielders of power. Nineteenth century England could with justice, but also with respect, be referred to as a "nation of shopkeepers". At the same time the peasant class was also being transformed. Millions of peasants throughout Europe moved from the farms to the towns to work for wages in the new industrial plants. The wages were poor, the hours long and the conditions of living deplorable. The factory workers provided the makings of a new class of society, the "working" class.

The industrial revolution brought wealth to the few but misery to the many. The depressed working class speedily found its spokesmen. On the one hand, there were the "ameliorationists", on the other hand the "revolutionists." The ameliorationists strove through legal procedure to improve working conditions, to increase wages, to reduce hours of work, to provide better housing and health services, to eliminate child labor. The ameliorationist policy has been pretty much that of the trade unions throughout the western world. The spokesmen for the revolutionists were Karl Marx (1818–83) and

Friedrich Engels (1820–95), two German radicals who had taken refuge in England. In 1848 they published the *Communist Manifesto,* and in 1867 Marx published *Das Kapital,* which were later to become respectively the Constitution and the Bible of the Communist movement. Marxism is a theory as well as a movement. The Marxist theory, insofar as it involves a doctrine of man, is a theory of economic determinism. It assumes that man is essentially a product of the economic conditions under which he has lived. Its political implication is that there will be an inevitable struggle between the two major classes of society, namely, the "exploiters" and "those who are exploited", that the workers will inevitably win and that there will ensue a classless society. The Communist movement has not always been faithful to Marxist theory, but we shall see how Marxist theory has had its influence in the shaping of contemporary psychology.

Political Democracy means that the votes of all men have equal weight under law. The battle for political democracy was gradually won in Great Britain during the eighteenth and nineteenth centuries, culminating in the concession of the vote to women. Western Europe and the Americas have tended to conform to the British pattern.

Social Democracy means that all people are *actually accepted* as equal. The most notable moves towards a social democracy have been in the Scandinavian countries and in the United States, and the battle is still far from won. The ideal of a social democracy is that every man (and woman), regardless of class, color of skin or religious creed should have an equal opportunity for advancement. The westward movement of European culture quickly broke down the barriers of class. Americans accepted people for "what they could do" rather than for "what their ancestors had been". A man who could "shoot straight" was accepted, whether or not he had a noble pedigree. A coward, whether or not he had a title, did not belong.

Religion created greater difficulties. The early American settlers were Puritan Protestants, Protestants who protested more against the Church of England than against the Church of Rome. The Protestant settlers of the New World were looking for a land in which they could be free to practice their religion. In the New England Colonies they achieved their freedom; but in the short space of a century they were persecuting deviants with no less ruthlessness than had the Spanish Inquisition persecuted its heretics. In 1692 a score of persons were hanged for witchcraft in Salem, Mass. On the whole, however, the religious movements that spearheaded the spread of the United States were essentially democratic in spirit. They may have been narrow in their theology and strict in their moral codes, but there was a measure of human fellowship in them. In a country that was battling to extend the frontier against the perils of nature the firmest faith was in the essential brotherhood of men.

The ideal of social democracy ran into difficulties, however, when it encountered the problem of race. The Europeans had few race problems, since there were few racial minorities. The Jews were always there as a minority group, who from time to time were brutally persecuted, but there were no great racial minorities distinguished by color of skin and texture of hair. It was in the New World that the "race" problem became acute. Hundreds of thousands of Blacks, mostly West Africans, had been brought over to work as slaves in the southern plantations. Obviously lacking in western culture, and apparently lacking in basic intelligence, they constituted a serious problem for the philosophers of social democracy. Even Thomas Jefferson, a convinced social democrat, had to twist his reasoning to find a place for the Blacks in God's scheme of things; and Abraham Lincoln, who battled valiantly for the rights of Blacks as human beings, was disturbed by their apparent lack of capacity. Even today it has not been fully demonstrated that "racial" lines are completely unrelated to intellectual capacity, but the evidence suggests that there is no necessary relation between the two. Even at the end of the nineteenth century, however, there were few dependable facts, and the defenders of social democracy had to rest pretty much on faith.

LITERATURE AND PHILOSOPHY IN THE
NINETEENTH CENTURY

Philosophy and literature in the nineteenth century is too rich to permit of a proper appraisal, even in the context of a merely psychological history. There are, however, few high lights, namely, (1) Post-Kantian transcendentalism, European and American; (2) literary romanticism; (3) the New World's faith in progress.

During the nineteenth century the gap between science and philosophy began to widen, and philosophy became progressively more and more closely allied with literature as one of the "humanistic" studies. A Bacon, a Descartes or a Leibnitz could lightly move from a study of empirical evidence to an examination of first principles, and even Kant could write voluminously on what would now be considered as scientific subjects. The Greek ideal of the philosopher as one who has mastered all knowledge could not, however, be sustained; science was uncovering more facts than any single mind could grasp and reflect upon. Philosophy was destined to become itself a specialized discipline, concentrating less on the ordering and integrating of knowledge than on the clarification of the principles that lie behind and beyond the world of observable fact. Kant's distinction between *phenomena* and *noumena* had much to do with this. The study of phenomena could be left to science; the philosopher's task was to explore the inner meaning of it all. A German historian of philosophy (Schwegler) could define his subject as "the thought totality of the empirical finite."

Kant launched the modern German idealistic movement that has baffled so many of its non-German students. Granted that the study of mere phenomena will never lead us to ultimate truth, can we achieve complete understanding through the exercise of pure reason? One after another the German philosophers—Fichte (1762–1814), Hegel (1770–1831), Schelling (1775–1854), Schopenhauer (1788–1860), and many others—presented reasoned interpretations of the universe that paid scant attention to the accumulating evidence of science. With meticulous logic, but in a jargon that tries the reader's patience, they removed the problems of philosophy so far from the realm of empirical verification that their arguments bore little relation to the concerns of everyday living, and could be quoted in support of almost any doctrine. Nietzsche (1844–1900), for instance, who thought he was an internationalist, was to be quoted with favor by the German National Socialists; and Karl Marx (1818–1883), who shared his dialectic method with Hegel, was to become the prophet of twentieth century Communism. German Transcendentalism "transcended" the problems of man and left man without practical guidance.

American Transcendentalism while less sophisticated, was closer to life. American transcendentalists, like Ralph Waldo Emerson

(1803–1882) and Henry David Thoreau (1817–1862), were *au courant* with the thinking of the European philosophers, but for them the challenge was to provide a philosophy of life for a new and developing country. They saw their brothers grubbing for a living among the stones of a rocky soil, or hitching their horses to a covered wagon that was to rumble across the unknown western plains. The pioneer's life keeps him close to the brute facts of nature, and his thinking does not ordinarily include much speculation about the nature of man and the universe. The New England transcendentalists were concerned lest their brothers lose their perspective. Transcendentalism, in New England, meant something more than an esoteric philosophy. It was an affirmation that there are values in life that transcend the ordinary motives of everyday living, and that these values should guide the nation that was coming into being. The New England Transcendentalists may have been fuzzy in their thinking, and prolix in their writing, but they helped to steer their country towards an ideal of itself, and consequently of man, that has left its imprint on man's conception of his role in society.

One of the best reflections of the nineteenth century is to be seen in the poetry, the art, the drama and the novels of the period. The century began in a mood of romantic revival, and it ended with its romanticism only slightly tempered by the realism that was to become so characteristic of the twentieth century. The romantic revival harks back to the days when wandering bards sang of the valorous exploits and the frustrated courtships of mythical heroes of a by-gone age. It represents an idealized interpretation of the past and of the life that is close to nature. In the nineteenth century it was a reaction against the cold and often cynical intellectualism that characterized the Age of the Enlightenment.

The early spokesman for the modern romantic movement was, of course, Rousseau with his ideal of the "noble savage" and his advocacy of a "return to Nature". Rousseau's influence is to be seen in the many attempts to found "utopias" (named after Thomas More's sixteenth century phantasy), ideal communities in which people will live close to nature and will consequently love one another. (One by one the utopias failed.) For the most part, however, the nineteenth century romanticists, while writhing under the constraints of a crude and materialistic society, and frequently impoverished because of their devotion, remained on the safe level of words, pictures, and music.

The greatest interpreter of the new romantic movement was un-doubtedly Johann Wolfgang von Goethe (1749–1832), poet, drama-tist, scientist and philosopher, who combined an interest in the world about him with a curiosity about principles that transcend the present. Within the compass of a few years, Goethe could publish one of the world's great dramatic analyses of the problem of human temptation (*Faust,* Part I, 1808), a heavy psychological novel (*Die Wahlverwandtschaften,* 1809), a vigorous attack on Newton's theory of color (*Zur Farbenlehre,* 1810); and his whole career is dotted with lyric poems, searching psychological analyses and profound philo-sophical disquisitions.

Historians refer to Goethe as the initiator of the period of *Sturm und Drang* (storm and stress) in literature. In the history of psychol-ogy he is a symbol of revolt against the domination of psychology by the methods and the constructs of the natural sciences. Goethe was a fairly good natural scientist, as well as a fairly good philosopher and a very great poet. Psychology's debt to him is not for his irascible attempt to disprove Newton's theory of color, but rather for his constant reminder that while natural science is one of the greatest of man's achievements, there are still things about man that natural science has not yet succeeded in explaining. Goethe's inspiration was to be felt in the nineteenth century movement that brought the phenomena of man's social and cultural life within the framework of a broadened conception of science.

For the most part, however, the romantic movement was alien to the spirit of science. Science was too dull and fact-grubbing for a Wordsworth, who could be moved to poetry by the sight of a field of daffodils, for a Keats who could recapture in brilliant verse the life depicted on a Grecian urn, or for a Byron, who could dramatize the life of Don Juan in impeccable cantos and then charge off to Greece to die in a futile attempt to give leadership to a hopeless revolution. The romantics were, in more recent terminology, "escapist." They sought an escape from the humdrum of everyday living in an idealiza-tion of nature, in the recapturing of the past, and in dreams of a perfect world of the future. Poets like Shelley and Storm, novelists like Scott, Stendhal and Hawthorne, and folklorists like Hans Ander-sen and the brothers Grimm looked to an idealized past for a picture of what man might become; and painters like Corot and Turner and musicians like Schumann and Mendelsohn gave color to the romantic ideal. The romantic movement was at its best in poetry, at its worst in philosophy. It was a combination of fine feeling and, possibly, muddled thinking; but it kept alive the realization that man possesses what in earlier terminology would have been called a "soul."

The romantic movement was destined to succumb to the grinding power of science and the brute realities of life in a competitive society. In the New World, however, idealism (in the practical rather than the Platonic sense) did not die. Just as oppression and slavery have always fostered the belief in a life-after-death, so the successful battle of the New World pioneers against nature's obstacles nourished a faith in a limitless future. One of the striking things about the mentality of the New World is the unquestioned assumption that what is to come will inevitably be better. The New World of the nineteenth century had become partially stabilized, agriculturally and industrially, but it still had open frontiers. Horace Greeley could quote "Go west, young man," as his advice to the young, and this meant literally that the West had unexploited resources. It also meant, metaphorically, that the future held out a promise to any man who possessed courage and initiative. As contrasted with the Old World, the New World offered the assurance of survival and the hope of "success". In the New World one might rise quickly from rags to riches. It is no accident that one of the least distinguished of American novelists, Horatio Alger, in all of whose stories the simple virtues of honesty and industry were unfailingly crowned with financial success, should have come to typify late nineteenth century America. Alger's books (he wrote more than 100 novels) were avidly read in Europe, but their effect was not to strengthen the virtues of honesty and industry but to increase the flow of immigrants to America.

The concept of "success" must be pondered as we look forward to the psychology of the nineteenth century. Success for Horatio Alger meant wealth and social position; and this conception of "success" is still prominent in American thinking. Interpreted more broadly, "success" means the achievement of that for which one is striving, and this in turn implies that that towards which one is striving is potentially realizable. In the Middle Ages the successful life was the life rewarded by eternal salvation; but this could not be verified scientifically. In the nineteenth century people wanted to achieve success in this world, and they believed that success could be demonstrated. They might demonstrate success by acquiring wealth, rising in the political hierarchy, winning a name as a scientist or artist, or gaining repute in the local community. We can readily understand why the Darwinian theory, with its picture of the upward struggle in nature and its implication that progress is inevitable, was to beat down the opposition of the orthodox. Darwinism, the great scientific revolution of the nineteenth century, was in tune with the nineteenth century faith in progress.

THE SCIENCES IN THE NINETEENTH CENTURY

It is the science of the nineteenth century, however, that will principally concern us, for during this century the study of man was to emerge as a science. During the nineteenth century the science of man was gradually taken over by those who were observing and measuring the cause and effect relationships in the physical world, the behavior of plants and animals, the structures and functions of the human body, and even the positions of the stars.

The philosophers still wrote about "psychology" as chapters or volumes in their philosophic systems, and we need not disparage their efforts. It was the scientists, however—Fechner, the physicist; Helmholtz, the physicist and physiologist; von Humboldt, the anthropologist and linguist; Darwin, the biologist—who were willing to look at human behavior and experience and try to derive scientific generalizations from their observations. The scientists of the nineteenth century were, for the most part, alive to the problems of the philosophers, but for them the discipline of scientific method was strong enough to place curbs on their curiosity. It may be that psychology accepted the discipline of science a little too soon; but, at any rate, it accepted the discipline enthusiastically. By the end of the century the "new psychology" of the laboratory was with mingled timidity and ostentation aping its colleagues in physics and biology and hoping that it would be recognized as a science.

The path that psychology was to tread was smoothed somewhat by the broadening conception of science in Germany. At the beginning. of the nineteenth century England and France were likely to identify "science" as mathematics and physics, with a possible grudging admission of chemistry and biology. The "social" sciences still belonged to philosophy. In Germany, however, the term *Wissenschaft*—equivalent to the Latin *scientia*—was extending its meaning. To be a *Wissenschaftler* was to be one who observed, classified, systematized, and interpreted the facts of any field of knowledge. There could consequently be the *Sozialwissenschaftler* (social scientist) and the *Naturwissenschaftler* (natural scientist), and there could be special branches of *Wissenschaft*, like *Sprachwissenschaft* (linguistics), *Literaturwissenschaft* (the study of literature) and even *Theaterwissenschaft* (the study of the theater). Science in Germany became the pursuit of exact knowledge in any field whatsoever.

The German university system favored this development. Germany had many more universities than either Great Britain or France, and there were consequently many more academic posts for scholars in Germany than elsewhere. In England or France the chance of obtaining a university professorship was so small as to discourage competition. In Germany the promising scholar had a chance, but to win in the competition he had to produce a work of scholarly worth. The pressure in Germany was consequently—as it still is—to produce something original, some new facts, a new theory, even a deviant opinion, anything that will distinguish the individual from his competitors. The would-be professor in a German university had to present a *Habilitationsschrift*, a major piece of research that went far beyond his doctoral thesis and that demonstrated his promise of leadership in his branch of learning. This was scrutinized by the best experts in the country, and the fortunate young man who received a favorable judgment was rewarded by the promise of a distinguished academic career. To be a professor in Germany was to rank high in the social hierarchy and to have the assurance of a better-than-average income. We can readily understand why in the Germany of the nineteenth century the best brains of the country were drawn into the *Wissenschaften*. And we can also understand why, because of the German insistence on originality, so many new disciplines should have been born. Among the new disciplines that sprouted in nineteenth century Germany was experimental psychology, a child of philosophy that was fostered by physiology. This could not have happened in France or England or the Americas, and it did not. Experimental psychology was born, and grew to maturity, within the German academic system.

During the nineteenth century the sciences, both in the English-French and in the German senses of the term, went forward by leaps and bounds. Discovery after discovery led to more refined techniques of observation and measurement, which in turn opened up new problems for investigation and new possibilities of application. A twentieth century commentator on the recent history of science could speak of "the romance of the next decimal place." A measurement could seem to be final; but the scientist always knew that lurking in the next decimal place there were unknowns that might upset all his theories. By the end of the century, long before the "atomic age," the scientist and the engineer (the two usually confused with one another) were beginning to be greeted with a reverence that in the Middle Ages was reserved for the priest. As science gradually broadened its scope to include the problems of man as well as those of animal life and the material world, there began to develop the faith that the world presents no problem that will not eventually yield to the methods of science.

The most notable developments were, of course, in the physical sciences, which had already received blueprint from Newton. The Newtonian scheme was not seriously modified, but the task of filling in the gaps was a challenge. The material world was still conceived as a composite of tiny indivisible material particles which could be combined in a great number of ways. Methods of calculating atomic weights were developed, and the Table of Elements, each with its own particular weight, was gradually filled in. It was found that most of the elements existed in compounds, some more stable than others, and that the interactions among compounds could be predicted and controlled in accordance with the atomic theory. The success of the new science of chemistry added strength to the Newtonian conception of the material world.

Even more dramatic was the discovery of electricity. The Italian Volta (volt = unit of electromagnetic force), the Frenchman Ampére (amp = unit of current) and the German Ohm (ohm = unit of resistance) had laid the groundwork for a new branch of physics. It was the Englishman, Michael Faraday (1791–1867), who unified their discoveries into a single theory and gave meaning to Newton's concept of force. After Faraday, the material world could no longer be considered as inert matter, but rather as a field of forces. Psychologists were slow in "catching up" with Faraday, but we shall see how the concept of "field" eventually found its place in psychological theory.

The biological sciences, slower in their start, were by the end of the century developing rapidly and were to open up a whole new approach to the study of man. Since the infancy of their science biologists had been constricted by the doctrine of the fixity of species. According to the account in Genesis each species of plant, fish, bird, and beast had been specially created with special forms and functions, and Aristotle and the Church had sanctified the doctrine. All the biologist could do was observe and classify the forms of plant and animal life and try to make each species meaningful in terms of the presumed purpose of God. In spite of these limitations, however, the biologists had accumulated a vast storehouse of descriptive information. The great Swedish botanist Linnaeus (1707–1778) is still respected for his studies of plant taxonomy; and the French paleontologist Cuvier (1769–1832) could marshall a wealth of observations and measurements in defense of the doctrine of special creation against the attacks of the new evolutionists.

The doctrine of evolution was, however, to win the day. That species can grow as individuals do had been suspected by the Greeks, but the church had discouraged such a belief. By the end of the eighteenth century the accumulating evidence in support of an evolutionary theory was becoming so strong that independently Charles Darwin's grandfather, Erasmus Darwin (1731–1802), and Goethe (1749–1832) could propose the theory that one species could gradually be transmuted into another. What was lacking was a specific explanation as to how such a transmutation can take place. The first bold suggestion was made by Lamarck (1744–1829). As the individual organism struggles to secure its food and protect itself against danger, he claimed, the bodily structures it uses are forced to develop in the direction of greater efficiency, and these structural changes are then transmitted through heredity to the next generation. Thus the giraffe acquired its long neck through constant stretching upward for the leaves on which it feeds, and the horse its protective hooves from galloping on stony ground. One might thus explain the gradual transformation of species in response to environmental changes. The Lamarckian theory is an optimistic one, in that it postulates a biological process whereby each generation can profit from the achievements of its predecessors. Unfortunately for the theory, how ever, the evidence is overwhelmingly against the inheritance of acquired characteristics. In some cultures, for instance, the rite of circumcision has been practiced for many centuries with no resultant structural change, and there is no reason to believe that generations of training in arithmetic have in any way improved the arithmetical ability of the race. From time to time a "Lamarckian" experiment in the laboratory has given promise of positive results, but none of these has been accepted by the most competent critics.

Charles Darwin's explanation of evolution was equally bold, but supported by much better evidence. Without completely rejecting the Lamarckian theory, he argued that the process of evolution can be better understood as a result of *natural selection.* All of life, he held, must be regarded as a struggle for survival, a struggle in which nature ruthlessly weeds out the misfits. Each species is characterized by certain structures and capacities which enable its individuals to adapt themselves to their environment. Thus the gills of the fish, the needles of the porcupine and the patterned skin color of the snake are adaptive structures, and the instincts of these animals are adaptive capacities or functions. If anything happens to change the environment or the individual in such a way that these structures and capacities are no longer adequate, then the struggle for survival is lost. The extinction of the dinosaurs is a familiar story. When the change is not too sudden or too drastic, however, species may survive through the development of new modes of adaptation; and this is the crux of the Darwinian theory. Let us look again at our giraffe.

In each generation of giraffes there are, purely by chance, some with longer and some with shorter necks. As long as the supply of food is plentiful, length of neck will bear no necessary relation to survival. If a shortage of food develops, however, the short necked animals will be the first to starve, and the next generation, produced by the longer necked animals, will tend to have longer necks. The basic Darwinian principles are thus: (1) spontaneous variation, (2) the selection by nature of those variations which prove to be adaptive, and (3) the transmission of these adaptive variations through heredity. Evolution is thus the result of a long, slow accumulation of minute changes that have accidentally appeared and that have proved to have survival value.

In its essentials the Darwinian theory has been fairly generally accepted, although many of its specific hypotheses have had to be corrected. It has been discovered, for instance, that the variations are not necessarily minute, nor are they always spontaneous. It seems probable that the most dramatic developments may be due to radical recombinations of genetic determinants (mutations), and that the occurrence of these mutations may actually be stimulated through the judicious manipulation of the environment. Genetics was not to become a science until after Darwin's time, and its sharpest tool, statistics, had not yet been created. Nevertheless, Darwin's conception of the evolutionary process was so radically new as to represent a revolution in science that was coordinate in importance with the revolutions of Newton and Copernicus. Darwin threw the intellectual world into turmoil, and out of the turmoil there emerged a new doctrine of man that was to give shape to the whole subsequent history of psychology.

While the biologists of the nineteenth century were bringing the world of plants and animals under the sovereignty of natural law, the students of the human organism—anatomists, physiologists, neurologists—were making equal progress towards the same end. The functioning of the human body was now becoming a science, and there was every reason to believe that the laws of natural science would eventually encompass man's mental as well as his physiological functions. By the end of the century man's optimism about the possibility of a "natural scientific" account of his own nature was unbounded.

The great names that will recur in our account are:

(1) Charles Bell (1774–1842), English physiologist, who independently of the French physiologist François Magendie (1783–1855), discovered the different functions of sensory and motor pathways in the nervous system. Their discovery is now known as the Bell-Magendie Law.

(2) Pierre Flourens (1794–1867), French anatomist and physiologist, stout battler against Phrenology, pioneer in the use of extirpation techniques, initiated the experimental movement in the study of brain loca'ization.

(3) Ernst Heinrich Weber (1795–1878), German anatomist and physiologist, made an exhaustive study of the "sense" of touch, and

quantified the relation between stimulus and sensation in a way that was later to provide the basis for the Weber-Fechner psychophysical principle.

(4) Johannes Müller (1801–1858) synthesized the physiology of his day in his great *Handbuch der Physiologie des Menschen* (1833–1840) and, among other original contributions, developed the Bell-Magendie law into the doctrine of the specific energies of nerves.

(5) Claude Bernard (1813–1878), one of the most famous of the nineteenth century French physiologists, recognized the principle of internal self-regulation in the organism that was much later to provide the basis for a physiological theory of motivation.

(6) Hermann von Helmholtz (1821–1894), physicist, physiologist and experimental psychologist did more than any other single individual to apply the experimental method to the solution of psychological problems. In his great works on *Physiological Optics* (1856–1866) and on the *Sensations of Tone* (1863) the new science of experimental psychology had its real beginning.

(7) Gustav Theodor Fechner (1801–1887), physicist, philosopher and quixotic genius conceived a theory of the mind-body relationship that was destined to founder, and a set of methods that were to become the mainstay of the new experimental movement. His *Elemente der Psychophysik* (1860) is sometimes regarded as heralding the birth of experimental psychology.

It is significant that most of these are German, that none was an ecclesiastic, and that all were university professors. Science in the nineteenth century was settling down to become a secular profession, centered in and supported by the universities, and more and more of the leadership was coming from Germany. The recent history of psychology includes a few clerics—like Brentano—but these were almost without exception university professors whose connection with the church was merely incidental. The growth of German leadership is a temptation to historical theorizing which we must resist. Suffice it to say that the world of science in the nineteenth century virtually belonged to Germany, as nineteenth century commerce and industry belonged to Britain. Until World War I, and even until the Hitler revolution, young scientists from all over the world flocked to the German universities for advanced training. Among these were young men who were eager to learn about the new psychology of the laboratory, many of them Americans. The psychology that was transplanted to the United States was essentially a German product.

The story of the social sciences must be postponed until later. The nineteenth century was not quite ready for a full-blown social science. Philosophers of democracy, like Rousseau, Thomas Paine, Benjamin Franklin, and Thomas Jefferson had looked forward to a science of social man. Explorers, missionaries, and colonizers had brought back tales of "the savages" and their queer customs and strange languages, and had suggested that, if the savages are to be converted and exploited, they must first be studied and understood. The agents of imperialism, military men and colonial administrators, found that it was not only expedient, but also interesting, to gain an understanding of the people under their control.

During the nineteenth century there accumulated a great store of practical information about the peoples of the world, most of it based on the casual reports of untrained observers. But these facts did not challenge the scientists, who were focused on the problems of physics and biology. True, there were some pioneers, like Herder (1744–1803), whose famous essay on the origin of language was to set the stage for a science of linguistics, and the von Humboldt brothers, Wilhelm (1767–1835) and Alexander (1769–1859), whose travels led them to examine the relation between man and his culture. On the whole, however, the social sciences had to await the stimulus of Charles Darwin. Comte (1798–1857) had presented a sociological program without substance. It was not until after Darwin that sociology, anthropology, and social psychology really began to find a foothold.

6

Associationism and Hedonism

THE NINETEENTH CENTURY gave us, in Associationism, the first consistent psychological theory of cognition of modern times. It had many great expositors, but the two greatest were James Mill (1773–1836) and Johann Friedrich Herbart (1776–1841). Mill drew upon the tradition of British empiricism, with its denial of inherent mental structure; and among his distinguished successors are Pavlov, Thorndike, Watson and Hull, the architects of modern behaviorism. Herbart's tradition was that of the rationalist Leibnitz, and we can recognize Herbartian themes in the dynamic psychologies of McDougall and Freud. Both Mill and Herbart believed that mental life could be explained by the association of ideas. For Mill the ideas were like the Newtonian particles of matter, bound together and operating in response to forces external to themselves. For Herbart the ideas contained their own force which governed their own combinations and conflicts. Before we examine these two types of associationism, however, we must make a distinction between the "principles" of association and associationism as a "theory."

ASSOCIATION AS PRINCIPLE AND AS THEORY

It was Aristotle, of course, who propounded the laws of association. He recognized the regularity in the flow of ideas, one idea arousing another in a meaningful way, and suggested that the ideas

179

were governed by four principles: similarity, contrast, contiguity in space and contiguity in time. The Aristotelian laws have subsequently been both amplified and simplified, but they have never been seriously challenged. The fact of association seems to be compelling. The question is whether the laws of association are sufficient to explain the structure and organization of mental life. The Associationists have held that such an explanation is possible.

In Aristotelian theory, and for many centuries after Aristotle, association was merely an ancillary principle. Association could explain the casual flow of ideas, but the laws that really bind the mental life into a unity were to be found in the indwelling purpose in the universe or in the transcendent purpose of God, either operating through a separate soul, or self. In Descartes, in Leibnitz, and even in the highly sophisticated thinking of Kant, we find the notion that the unity of mental life is not a mere product of chance associations but the reflection of a more stable, transcendent order. Rationalism has always had a place for the laws of association, but it has never accepted associationism as a theory.

Associationism as a theory developed in the context of British empiricism. Hobbes was in his way an associationist, and so were Locke, Berkeley, and Hume. To understand a theory one must always try to grasp what it is trying to explain and what it is pitted against. The early British empiricists were living in a physical world that was gradually being described and explained in terms of physical law; they were pitted against a theological tradition (Protestant as well as Roman Catholic) that still believed in angels, devils, and miracles, that withheld the realm of mind from scientific study; they wanted to find through the study of human nature a set of laws, analogous to those of physical science, that would not only explain the phenomena of mind in a "natural" way but also provide a guide for human conduct. The laws they found were the laws of association.

Long before James Mill began to write, David Hartley (1705–1757) had elevated the principle of association to the status of a theory. Hartley, an English physician, strongly influenced by Newton and Locke, had argued that the ideas in the mind paralleled the miniature vibrations in the brain and that ideas or vibrations that occur together or in succession become so linked that the occurrence of one leads to the arousal of those that have been associated with it.

Hartley's was both a parallelist and an associationist theory. The Scottish School, Thomas Reid (1710–1796), Dugald Stewart (1753–1828) and Thomas Brown (1778–1820), had begun as antiempiricist and had ended with an almost frank associationism. Reid opposed the philosophic scepticism of Hume and the physiological theorizing of Hartley on grounds of "common sense", asserting that the human mind possesses certain God-given faculties or powers that must be simply taken for granted. Brown, a disciple of Stewart, who was a disciple of Reid, loyally rejected the terminology of association theory but substituted for "association" the completely equivalent term "suggestion". Brown's laws of suggestion are, as a matter of fact, among the best of the early statements of associationist theory.

JAMES MILL AND THE MECHANICAL PRINCIPLE

It was James Mill, however, who gave us the classic associationist analysis of human mentality. With Hume, the "soul" of man had evaporated and the existence of a human "mind" had been called into question. With Mill the "mind" itself dissolved into arrays, complexes and successions of ideas. Mill's analysis of human mentality is the best example we have of a psychology fashioned after the pattern of Newtonian physics.

James Mill, a Scotsman, was groomed for the clergy, but speedily discovered that he had no gift for preaching and moved to the more precarious field of writing. He is best known as historian, as political economist, and as the tutor of his brilliant son, John Stuart Mill. As a logically minded psychologist, however, he ranks with the best. His *Analysis of the Phenomena of the Human Mind* (1829) may have been misguided, but it is still one of the clearest expositions of associationist theory that we have.

The Newtonian universe was composed of material elements bound together by forces and behaving in a predictable way. It would seem plausible that the phenomena of the human mind could in like fashion be analyzed into their elements, and the modes of combination and interaction among these stated as psychological laws. This, at any rate, was the hope of the associationists. Mill's associationism gives us: (1) an inventory of the elements of mind, (2) a formulation of the laws of combination and interaction, and (3) a demonstration that all mental phenomena can be explained in this way. Just as the material universe is nothing more than its component physical elements, so the "mind" is nothing more than its component mental elements. James Mill's analysis followed the analogy of Newtonian mechanics. His son, John Stuart Mill (1806–1873), felt that the facts of chemical fusion provided a better analogy, and Herbert Spencer (1820–1903) gave the theory an evolutionary setting. All were at one, however, in their insistence that mind can be reduced to its elements and thereby explained. All subsequent associationist theories have maintained the same faith.

What are the elements of mind? For James Mill there are two kinds of mental element: sensations and their copies, ideas. All mental life can be explained in terms of the orderly associations among these. Let us consider in turn the sensations, the ideas, and the principles of association.

Aristotle had imposed a fivefold classification of the senses, albeit with some reservations about the complexity of the sense of touch, each sense providing its own unique type of sensation. For the associationists it was important that the primary types of sensation be identified and, as we shall see, one of the lively interests of nineteenth century physiology was in the search for new sense organs. James Mill accepted Aristotle's primary five senses, but added three more. In addition to sight, hearing, taste, smell and touch, he argued, there are: a muscular sense (previously identified by Thomas Brown), a sense of disorganization (revealed in the experience of itches and tickles) and an alimentary sense (responsible for such feelings as hunger, nausea, and general well-being). Together, the eight senses provided the raw material out of which mind was constructed. We shall later consider the meaning of "the senses" (cf. chapter 7). So far as the associationists were concerned the senses were separate mechanisms whereby unique sensations were produced. Each sense transmitted its own proper sensations, and these were the building blocks with which the structure of mind was fashioned.

Ideas, according to Mill, are copies of sensations. They may be simple ideas, like the image of a color that we have recently sensed, although the idea need not be weaker than the sensation, as Hume had affirmed. More commonly, however, the ideas come as complexes of sensations that have been bound together into a unity, like the idea of a tree, which combines color (visual), form (visual and tactual), surface characteristics (visual and tactual), resilience (muscular), and even smell. In current terminology this would be labelled a percept. What is important is that for the associationists a percept is a complex idea that is reducible to simpler ideas, and eventually to sensations. Equally important, however, is the associationist claim that, just as simple ideas can be combined into complex ideas, so complex ideas can be combined into still more complex ideas. Thus, to use one of Mill's examples, the idea of chair is a combination of simple ideas of color, shape, texture, rigidity, etc., but when we combine it with the ideas of table, footstool, bookcase and lamp we have the still more complex idea of furniture. And the complex idea of furniture can be combined with other complex ideas to produce the most complex idea of all, namely, the idea of Everything. Thus, the superstructure of mind consists of very general ideas, each of which contains a cluster of complex ideas, all reducible to simple ideas, and all finally reducible to elementary sensations. This is a model of the mind that matches the Newtonian model of the physical world.

But what about the forces that hold the mental world together and make it operate? Is there any psychological law that can match the Newtonian law of gravitation? For James Mill the parallel was to be found in the law of association. Sensations and ideas were connected through association just as material particles were held together by the force of gravity. To explain the unity of mind one need postulate nothing more than a number of elements and a set of laws in accordance with which the elements are combined.

Aristotle's laws of association had included similarity, contrast, and spatial and temporal contiguity. In Mill's thinking these all boiled down to temporal contiguity, supported by secondary conditions (listed by Thomas Brown) like frequency, recency and vividness. "Table" suggests "chair," not because tables and chairs are similar, but because they regularly occur together; similarly for "black" and "white". "Pen" and "ink" are spatially contiguous, but they would not have been associated had they not been together in time. For Mill the temporal factor was the crucial condition for association.

More important than the specific conditions of association, however, is the assertion that ideas are elements of mind and that these elementary ideas are the constituents of all the complex states and processes of mental life. Mill distinguished between synchronous and successive associations, e.g., between the blending of visual and tactual sensations into the percept of a chair and the almost compulsive sequential association of chair with table. Perceived objects are the products of synchronous association, trains of thought the evidence of successive association. The appeal of Mill's associationism is that it promised a "mechanics of mind" that might match the mechanism of Newtonian physics. Mill carried his analysis through, explaining in terms of the mechanical combination of mental elements such processes as memory, imagination, conceptualization and linguistic symbolism, and even offering an associationist basis for human motivation (p. 188).

A CRITIQUE OF ASSOCIATIONISM

Seldom has a neater psychological system been presented; and those who like neatness above all things should find Mill fully satisfying. There are, however, two interrelated objections to mechanical associationism, both of which are still pertinent. These are:

(1) A merely mechanical model cannot adequately represent the complexity of human experience. This objection was actually made by Mill's own son. John Stuart Mill (1806–1873) was impressed by the fact that chemical compounds have properties that are not recognizable in the elements from which they are compounded. An examination of a compound, like water, does not tell anything about hydrogen or oxygen. Newton had shown how white light was a compound of all the spectral colors. It could be, suggested John Stuart Mill, that there are mental combinations that resemble the chemical as well as those that resemble the mechanical. The elementary ideas compounded through "mental chemistry" may be really there, but they may not be recognized. John Stuart Mill may have been simply advancing the psychological analogue from physics to chemistry. Whether or not he recognized it, however, he was implicitly challenging the assumption that psychological analysis must conform to the accepted pattern of the physical sciences.

(2) Logical implication must not be confused with psychological content. The criticism is that James Mill's analysis is essentially

logical rather than psychological. Some examples might help to clarify the point. Given a right-angled triangle, we can demonstrate that the square of the hypotenuse equals the sum of the squares of the two remaining sides (the theorem of Pythagoras). We know that one divided by zero equals infinity. When we travel eastward from one time zone to the next we accept the requirement that we advance our watches by one hour. Having insured the contents of our house against theft, we are not astonished to discover that this particular article is covered by the insurance. In each case we have a consequence that is logically implied by certain antecedent facts or premises. But does this logically demonstrable relationship necessarily represent what takes place in the thinking of the individual? The theorem of Pythagoras requires an intricate proof, and many an engineer uses the theorem even after he has forgotten the proof. The concept of undivided unity strains the imagination; it is much easier just to remember the formula. How many people immediately grasp the relation between the movement of the earth and the position of the sun when they advance their watches? And how many householders literally think of each individual article when they insure their furniture? True, the concept of furniture *implies* this table, this chair, and this lamp, plus other articles that have not yet been purchased, but these do not have to be psychologically present when one thinks of furniture, any more than the various steps in the Pythagorean demonstration have to be psychologically present when one makes use of the theorem.

The "idea of furniture" was one of Mill's own examples, and we can readily see in it a confusion of logic with psychology. His "idea of Everything" is even more baffling, for it would require the simultaneous presence of all possible ideas. In the language we have been using, Mill's "idea" is not a datum but a construct. It is not an identifiable phenomenon but a hypothetical entity that has been logically inferred. Mill's psychology begins with an attempt to describe faithfully the properties of immediate experience, but it develops rapidly into a system in which the "ideas" are merely the psychological analogues of Newton's particles of matter.

Mill's Associationism is a model for "empirical theory," in that it reduces mental life to hypothetical mental units and provides the simplest possible set of rules whereby these units are combined. In this sense Mill was more successful than were any of his empiricist predecessors, even more successful than Hume. Subsequent associationists have changed the terminology (e.g., to conditioned reflexes, S–R bonds), but Mill's model is still recognizable. As an example of the "empirical approach," however, Mill's psychology is unsatisfactory. He tried to look at human experience and make a science out of it; but he was bound by the Newtonian conception of science, and the centuries of Aristotelian logic that lay behind him constrained him to thrust the phenomena into traditional categories rather than to see them as they are.

HERBART AND THE CONCEPTION OF MENTAL DYNAMICS

On the Continent another kind of Associationism was being advanced. Herbart (1776–1841) shared with the physical scientists a zeal for quantification and with the British empiricists the desire to reduce psychology to a science like physics; but he was also under the influence of the rationalism of Leibnitz, and he succeeded Kant in the chair of philosophy at Königsberg. Among his many published works the most important for psychology is his *Psychologie als Wissenschaft, neugegründet auf Erfahrung, Metaphysik und Mathematik*, 1824–25 (psychology as science, newly founded on experience, metaphysics and mathematics). Herbart is better known as a pioneer in educational theory, but we shall see how his theory of education rests on certain psychological principles.

Leibnitz had held that the universe is composed of an infinite number of active elements, each with its own minuscule consciousness. Herbart borrowed the notion of activity from Leibnitz, and the concept of the "idea" from the British empiricists. Herbart's "idea" was an active element of mind, like a physical particle imbued with energy and consciousness. He agreed with the British empiricists in asserting that there is no independent entity that can be termed a "soul" or a "mind"; but he insisted that mental processes are dynamic, *i.e.*, that ideas have force. Newton's particles of matter possessed no intrinsic force, and Mill's "ideas" were like Newton's material elements, which could be pushed about by extraneous forces. Herbart's "ideas" contained their own energy and could steer their own combinations.

Like James Mill, Herbart was an empiricist in that he denied special mental faculties and tried to reduce mental complexes to simple ideas; unlike Mill, he considered the mind, albeit an integration of ideas, as capable of organizing, directing and regulating its own contents. The key to his system is the concept of the "apperception mass." Compatible ideas cluster themselves into units (the apperception mass) and combine their forces to determine which new ideas will be incorporated and which will be thrust out of consciousness. Here is a simple-minded example. If we combine the ideas of "about three feet long," "straight," "made of wood," "useful for measurement," we have the idea of yardstick; to add the idea "yellow" merely makes it a yellow yardstick. Let us add another idea, "having only one end," and what happens? A yellow yardstick with only one end is nonsense; either the original idea collapses or the new idea is rejected. Thus, with all mental processes, the existing apperception mass determines the extent to which new ideas can be assimilated. The implications of this for education are obvious, and one understands why Herbart ranks so high among educational theorists.

But this is only part of the story. An idea that is thrust out of consciousness because it is incompatible with the existing apperception mass is not lost. Nothing is ever completely forgotten. Below the threshold of consciousness are innumerable rejected ideas awaiting readmission or awaiting the mobilization of their weakened forces. Think, for example, of the time when the earth was believe to be flat. The movements of the sun, the moon, and the stars required some explanatory ingenuity, but the common sense belief was not seriously challenged. Gradually, however, evidence supporting a different hypothesis grew more and more convincing. In Herbartian terms, the rejected ideas mobilized their forces and eventually shattered the existing apperceptive mass. Today, the notion that the earth is spherical is part of the common apperceptive mass. Any incompatible idea would be promptly rejected. With Herbart, the notion of "the unconscious" begins to loom as important.

Is there a threshold which unconscious ideas must cross before they become conscious. Herbart gave us the concept of the *limen* (threshold) as the dividing line between the conscious and the unconscious, a concept that was to figure largely in the later psychophysics.

HEDONISM

HEDONISM dominated the nineteenth century theory of motivation until Darwin, just as associationism dominated the theory of cognition; in fact, they are part and parcel of the same Newtonian doctrine of man. Nineteenth century hedonism extends the associationist principle to include the explanation of human conduct. Added to elementary sensations and ideas are simple feelings of pleasure and pain which, combined with ideas, produce action. An idea that threatens pain is rejected; an idea that promises pleasure is supported. Pleasure and pain are the initiators, the regulators and the directors of behavior. "Nature ," said Jeremy Bentham, "has placed mankind under the governance of two sovereign masters, pain and pleasure. It is for them alone to point out what we ought to do, as well as to determine what we shall do." For Bentham and his followers the hedonistic principle was both an explanation of and a guide for conduct.

ETHICAL *VS.* PSYCHOLOGICAL HEDONISM

Two types of hedonism are usually recognized. (1) According to *ethical hedonism* the attainment of pleasure and the avoidance of pain are man's ethical goals. We *ought to* govern our lives by this simple principle. (2) *Psychological hedonism* begs the ethical question but asserts that in fact people do govern their lives in accordance with the pleasure-pain principle. Psychological hedonism can again be subdivided into (a) a teleological and (b) a causal hedonism. According to *teleological* hedonism there is a natural goal towards which all behavior is directed. This goal may be set by a purpose that lies behind nature (transcendent teleology), like God's purpose in the creation of the universe, or it may be an indwelling purpose that is gradually fulfilled in the process of evolution (immanent teleology). In either case it is assumed that all behavior is pointed towards the attainment of pleasure, or happiness, and away from pain. According to the *causal* principle, the direction of behavior is regulated by its pleasurable or painful consequences. Acts that lead to pleasure tend to be repeated; those that produce pain are suppressed.

When we examine hedonism as a theory of human conduct it is important that we keep in mind the distinction between the ethical and the psychological problem. For the great hedonistic thinkers, and Jeremy Bentham is the best of them, ethics and psychology could not be divorced from one another. What ought to be must be grounded in what is. Bentham was a great humanitarian. He felt the misery into which the industrial revolution was precipitating his fellowmen. He resented the doctrine of the afterlife that offered a compensation for this world's suffering. What he demanded was a society in which people could be comfortable and happy.

Psychologists have sometimes argued that all problems of ethics will eventually be restated as problems of science, to be solved by empirical methods. From this point of view, what people *ought* to do can be determined in the light of what they are and of the forces that play upon them at any given time. This, however, is a question that cannot be answered here. The important historical fact is that from time immemorial men have sought for a psychological basis for their own ethical judgments. Hedonism is the best example of this quest, and it was the hedonistic approach that appealed to the Newtonian world of the nineteenth century.

7

The "New" Psychology

of the Laboratory

BY THE BEGINNING of the nineteenth century the experimental movement had thoroughly conquered the sciences of physical nature and had penetrated deeply into the study of life processes. Philosophers were still speculating about the nature of "the mind" but, as we have seen, were already gearing their speculations to the concepts of the natural sciences. It was the scientists, however, who proceeded to study the phenomena of mind as they were studying the phenomena of nature. Hume and Kant had demonstrated logically that an empirical science of mind was impossible. The scientists, fortunately, were unimpressed by metaphysical impossibilities; they were simply curious about the phenomena of consciousness and were eager to know how these could be related causally to the familiar facts of physics and biology. It was the old mind-body problem that fascinated them, but now restated in the context of the new science. What later was labeled the "new" science of psychology was an incidental creation of physicists, anatomists, physiologists, neurologists, and even astronomers, who were indeed alive to the traditional problems of metaphysics but who saw no reason why the phenomena of mind should not be observed, analyzed and measured according to the methods that were proving so useful in the other fields.

It was not until late in the nineteenth century that psychology was explicitly labeled as an experimental science, and not until very much later that it began to be recognized as a legitimate university department. The story of psychology's emergence as a science is

191

consequently rooted in the history of sciences that were not explicitly concerned with psychological problems. Bell, Magendie, and Johannes Müller are known best for their contributions to physiology; Fechner was a physicist, with a passionate interest in metaphysics; Helmholtz was a physicist who moved from physics to physiology to psychology; Wundt was a philosopher in the old sense of the term, curious about everything, who was entranced by the sciences of nature and proceeded to design an experimental science of mind. Wundt published his first major psychological work in 1873, and in 1879 established the world's first psychological laboratory. Whether or not he or Fechner should be listed in history as the father of experimental psychology is immaterial; it was Wundt who founded the laboratory, who attracted the students from far and wide, and who sent his students to all parts of the western world to establish new psychological laboratories.

From Bell to Wundt the story belongs mostly to the biological sciences, with strong support from physics. The mind-body problem, as the Newtonian scientists saw it, begins with the material world. The material world consists of particles in various spatial and temporal configurations. How are these reflected in consciousness? Locke's distinction between primary and secondary qualities was altogether too simple, and Berkeley had demolished it. The scientists began to look at the particulars. Granted a physical world, which the scientists did not question, how does it generate ideas of itself? Obviously, first, by specially receptive organs which respond differentially to the varying dimensions of the physical world; and the scientists began to look for specialized receptors. How do the receptors transmit their information? Obviously we must know something about the conducting mechanism, and this became a central scientific concern. What happens when the impulse has been conducted from the receptor to the central portions of the brain? Obviously the secrets of the brain will have to be unlocked; and the attempt to do this yielded one of the most exciting chapters in the history of nineteenth century science. And, finally, how does the activity in the brain centers become channeled into consciousness and action?

These, then, were the specific questions to which the mind-body problem was reduced and which the nineteenth century scientists undertook to solve: (1) the mechanism of sense-reception; (2) the mechanism of nerve conduction; (3) the mechanisms of the brain;

and (4) the mechanisms of action and reaction. In each case the scientist was looking for correlations: between physical events and sensory events, between sensory events and brain functions, between brain functions and overt actions, and between all of these and consciousness. Each of these questions deserves special treatment.

Aristotle had recognized five senses: vision, hearing, smell, taste, and touch; James Mill added some more. By the nineteenth century the sanctity of the Aristotelian classification had begun to fade, and scientists were beginning to ask exactly how many "gateways to the mind" there actually were, how they could be identified, and how they functioned. The question they did not always stop to ask was: what do we mean by "a sense"? And this question, we find, is easier to ask than to answer. Are the senses to be classified in terms of physical stimuli, in terms of anatomical structures, or in terms of the qualities of experience? Much of the confusion in nineteenth century research is due to the fact that the criteria whereby "a sense" can be identified were never fully agreed upon.

The Aristotelian classification seems at first glance to be simple and obvious. We have eyes, ears, a nose, a tongue, and a skin. These are the channels whereby we maintain contact with the outside world. But the eyes provide us with blacks and whites, reds and blues; the tongue with sweets and sours, and so forth, and, as Mill pointed out, the muscles and the alimentary tract provide us with still other types of sensation. It would appear that each of Aristotle's senses will have to be broken down into a list of subsenses, each responsible for its own particular kind of sensation, and each identified as a special anatomical structure. And this, in fact, is what happened in the nineteenth century. Much of the sensory physiology and psychology of that period proved to be an avid, but often tedious, search for sense organs.

Another simple and obvious approach is to disregard the sense organs temporarily, to classify the variables of the physical world which are reflected in experience, and then to ask how this representation takes place. It might be argued that, since our sensory systems have developed in response to the physical environment, there ought to be an identifiable sense corresponding to each of the basic types of physical process. The senses ought accordingly to be classified in terms of physical stimuli. At first glance this, too, seems plausible. In the physical sciences we study such problems as: light, sound, heat, electricity, gravitation, mechanical propulsion and chemical change. For most of these we obviously have senses: eyes for light, ears for sound, tongues and noses for chemical stimulation, and the skin for most of the others. Aristotle had no sense corresponding to gravitational pull, and he knew nothing of electricity; but these merely present an additional challenge to research, a challenge which in the case of gravitation led to the discovery of the receptor structures of the inner ear.

This approach dominated much of nineteenth century research on sensation, and indeed still characterizes much of contemporary psychophysics and psychophysiology. The physically oriented scientist could not, of course, rest content with a simple "light sense" or "sound sense" or "chemical sense." Newton had demonstrated, for instance, that "white" light can be broken down into an array of spectral components, ranging from red to violet, corresponding to which there must be special sensory processes responsive to the different wave lengths of light. Similarly sound is physically a set of vibrations varying in frequency, requiring corresponding sensory structures to give us the range of tones we hear; and the chemical difference between an acid and a base, since it is sensed, must be represented by different chemical receptors. It is clear that a primarily physical classification of the senses leads, as indeed it did, to the conclusion that there are many more senses than the original five.

Appealing as the anatomical and physical principles of classification are, they break down quickly when we begin to look at the facts. Colors are not dependent solely on stimulation of the eye; a bump on the head, as every ice skater knows, may produce a fine array of colors. Nor can any color be coordinated exclusively to a particular wave length of light; in any elementary psychological laboratory it is regularly demonstrated that a pale but respectable red can be produced through the fusion of wave lengths, far apart in the spectrum, colloquially designated as orange and violet; and all psychologists know that there is no wave length corresponding to purple. The same holds true for other senses. Sensations of warm and cold, for instance, correspond to gradients of stimulation rather than to absolute temperatures. In the familiar demonstration in which the two hands are immersed for a period, one in warm and the other in cold water, and both are then plunged into tepid water, the tepid water feels cold to the one and warm to the other. It is clear that the senses cannot be classified simply on the basis of physical stimulation and receptor reaction.

In spite of the inadequacy of the physical and anatomical classifications, the fact remains that colors, sounds, tastes, smells and pressures have from time immemorial been recognized as different kinds of experience, and that these very differences in experience invite the hypothesis of differentiated senses. In the last analysis it is the uniqueness of a particular kind of experience that dictates its ascription 'to a corresponding sense. Sights and sounds were recognized as different kinds of sense long before anything was known of light waves and sound waves or of the anatomy and physiology of the retina and the inner ear. An interesting fact is that today we identify warm, cold, pain and pressure as different types of sensation, but we have not yet fully specified the physical stimuli which arouse them, and we are quite unclear as to which structures function as receptors. In other words, we have recognized the sensation and are now *looking for* the stimuli and the receptors.

The concept of "a sense" as a differentiated system, responding by means of particular anatomical structures to particular physical stimuli and yielding a particular kind of sensation, has consequently lost much of its status in psychological theory and is gradually being replaced by more sophisticated notions. In the nineteenth century, however, the Aristotelian doctrine was not seriously challenged. The scientists implicitly accepted the phenomenological criterion, but their explicit purpose was to identify receptors and to measure the stimuli which arouse them. It is perhaps a good thing that they did not spend too much time psychologizing. There were innumerable concrete problems to be solved, which they attacked with skill and patience; what little psychologizing they did has left us with a heritage of error and confusion from which we have not yet become completely disentangled.

The main explorations were, understandably, into the "senses" of vision and hearing; but there was also important pioneering in taste, smell and touch, and in other fields, such as kinaesthesis, not included in Aristotle's five senses. As we glance at the major findings in the various fields we must remember that there was little questioning of the traditional concept of "the senses". The scientists, for the most part, believed in a "real" world which somehow or other conveyed information about itself through the senses to the "mind" of the knower. Their task was to identify the mechanism whereby the transmission takes place. Most of them were willing to leave questions about "the mind" to the philosopher.

Appendix

The table of contents of the intended volume is listed below. An instructor who wishes to build his course in the history of psychology on the structure provided by Professor MacLeod will find this outline indispensable.

The Darwinian revolution and its consequences
    Darwinian concepts, restated in psychological terms
    the comparative study of species
    individual development and differentiation
    social man as a product of evolution
    mechanism vs. vitalism

Influences from the medical clinic
    a backward glance at the history of mental disorder
    the new conception of mental disorder as disease
    the challenge from hypnotism
    the French schools of psychotherapy: Salpetriere vs. Nancy
    systematology vs. dynamic psychology: Kraepelin vs. Freud
    the concept of the "normal"

William James' restatement of the persistent problems
    mind and body
    the basis of cognition
    the basis of conduct
    man as a social being

PART IV.

Recent Trends in Psychological Thinking

A preview of twentieth century developments
    university systems in Europe and the USA
    shifting centers of political and economic power

World War I and its consequences for psychology
the period between the wars
World War II and its consequences for psychology

Psychology attempts to become objective
the new conception of behavior
Pavlov and the conditioned reflex
Watson's behaviorist manifesto
operationism in physics and psychology
the psychology of the "empty organism"—Skinner
the mathematico—deductive method—Hull
strengths and weaknesses of behaviorism

Consciousness revived and revised
the psychologies of act and content
psychological phenomenology and existentialism
the psychology of "understanding"
Ganzheit and *Gestalt*—the holistic psychologies
theories of the psychological "field"
a re-assessment of the concept of consciousness

Psychology probes the unconscious
pre-Freudian conceptions of the unconscious
Freud's theory of the neuroses
Freud's theory of the person
Freud's deviating disciples: Adler, Jung, Rank
Freud's emancipated disciples: Horney, Fromm, Sullivan
a re-assessment of Freud's challenge to psychology

Reconciliations
Behaviorism, McDougall, Freud, Gestalt theory—Tolman
Freud, Gestalt theory—Lewin
Behaviorism, Freud—Miller and Dollard
can psychological theory be unified?

Psychology becomes practical
the contribution of practice to theory and of theory to
    practice
psychology in education
psychology in industry
psychology in the court of law

psychology in the medical clinic
what is the relevance of psychological theory to the
  currently developing psychological professions?

A new look at some old problems
  the meaning of individuality
  psychology and ethical judgment
  psychology and aesthetic judgment
  opinion, belief and knowledge
  communication
  is man a machine?

Index

201

Rousseau, Jean Jacques, 115, 138,
    147–151, 153, 168, 177
Royce, J.R., 4n, 6n
Rubens, Peter Paul, 117
Russell, Bertrand, 96, 127, 144
Ryan, T., 2

Saint-Just, 149
Sartre, Jean-Paul, 78
Sceptic and scepticism, 34, 50
Schelling, F.W.J. von, 146, 167
Schopenhauer, Arthur, 146, 167
Schumann, Robert, 169
Schwegler, 167
Science, 5, 17
    meaning of, 101–108
    nineteenth century, 171–78
    of psychology, 6, 143–146
    and religion, 156
    qua Science, 15
Scientific attitude, meaning of, 17–18
Scott, 169
Shakespeare, William, 89, 101, 117
Shelley, Percy Bysshe, 169
Sherif, C., 12n
Sherif, M., 7n, 12n
Sixteenth century, background of,
    87–91
Skinner, B.F., 198
Smith, Adam, 115, 147, 150–52
    An Inquiry into the Nature and
        Causes of the Wealth of Nations,
        150
    Theory of Moral Sentiments, 151
Socio-economic classes, 22–23
Socrates, 2, 17, 57–58, 60, 72, 75, 77,
    102, 108
Sophists, 48–49, 57
Sophocles, 58
Spencer, Herbert, 182

Spinoza, Baruch, 112, 119, 122, 128
    Ethics, 119
Stendhal, 169
Stewart, Dugald, 181
Stoics, 72
Storm, 169
Sullivan, Harry Stack, 198

Tschaikowsky, 39
Teleological principle, 66. See also
    Classic doctrines of man,
    teleological
Thales, 47
Theaetetus, 17
Thoreau, Henry David, 168
Thorndike, 179
Titian, 117
Tolman, 198
Troland, L.T., 127
    The Mystery of Mind, 127
Turner, 169

Van Dyck, Anthony, 117
Vermeer, 117
Vesalius, Andreas, 9, 100
Victoria (Queen of England), 162–63
Villon, François, 89
Vinci, Leonardo da, 9, 92, 100, 117
    "The Last Supper," 92
    "Mona Lisa," 92
Volta, Alessandro, 173
Voltaire, 115, 120, 127, 133, 138,
    149, 153
    Candide, 120, 127

Wann, T.W., 4n
Watson, John B., 179, 198
Weber, Ernst Heinrich, 176–77
Wertheimer, M., 2n
Wilberforce, William, 164

Wolff, Christian von, 131, 142–44, 151
  Psychologia Rationalis, 142
  Von Gott, der Welt und der Seele des Menschen, auch allen Dingen überhaupt, 142n

Wordsworth, William, 169
Wundt, Wilhelm, 192

Yahweh, 72–73